AGILE LEADERSHIP

MASTERING TRUST, EMPATHY,
AND EMPOWERMENT FOR
ORGANIZATIONAL SUCCESS

DR. KEVIN DUFFY

Agile Leadership:
Mastering Trust, Empathy, and Empowerment for Organizational Success

Dr. Kevin Duffy

ISBN: 9798301056086

Cover Design: Catherine Corcoran

Publication Year: 2024

Publisher: Independently Published via Amazon Direct

Copyright © 2024 Dr. Kevin Duffy. All rights reserved.

No part of this book may be reproduced, distributed, or transmitted in any form or by any means, including photocopying, recording, or other electronic or mechanical methods, without the prior written permission of the author, except in the case of brief quotations embodied in critical reviews and certain other noncommercial uses permitted by copyright law.

This book is a work of non-fiction. The author has made every effort to ensure the accuracy of the information contained within, but it is provided for informational purposes only. The author and publisher assume no responsibility for errors, omissions, or the interpretation of the material presented.

For permissions or inquiries, contact: www.drkevinduffy.com

Printed in the United States of America.

Amazon Direct Publishing Edition

Dedication

To my wife, Colleen Duffy, and my two incredible children, Macayla Duffy and Kevin Duffy—your love, support, and encouragement inspire me to be better every day. Your patience and sacrifice have given me the time and space to pursue my passion, and without you, this book would not have been possible. You are my greatest motivation, and everything I do is for you.

To my parents, Kevin Duffy and Jami Lee Duffy, whose unwavering guidance and values shaped the foundation of my character. The lessons you instilled in me have given me the strength, determination, and resilience to thrive in all aspects of life.

To my brother, Dr. Sean Duffy, whose pursuit of excellence in education and professional growth inspired me to embark on my own journey in project management. Your ambition and dedication continue to push me toward greater achievements.

This book is a testament to the support, love, and wisdom I have received from each of you. I am forever grateful.

"True leadership is not measured by authority, but by the trust you build, the empathy you show, and the empowerment you inspire."

— Dr. Kevin Duffy

Table of Contents

Preface 1

Foreword 3

Introduction: The Need for Agile Leadership 5

Chapter 1: What is Agile? 13

Chapter 2: Why Leaders Struggle with Agile 29

Chapter 3: Servant Leadership 39

Chapter 4: Building Agile Teams 49

Chapter 5: Fostering a Culture of Agility 61

Chapter 6: Measuring Success and Sustaining Agile Transformation 73

Chapter 7: Overcoming Challenges in Agile Transformation 87

Chapter 8: Agile Tools and Technologies 101

Chapter 9: Sustaining Agile Momentum 117

Chapter 10: Future-Proofing Agile Practices 131

Chapter 11: Trust as the Foundation of Leadership 145

Chapter 12: Leading with Empathy 157

Chapter 13: Empowerment as a Leadership Imperative 171

Chapter 14: Becoming a TEE Leader 185

APPENDIX 191

References 203

Appendix: Lifelong Learning in Agile Leadership 206

About the Author 213

Glossary of Terms 215

Preface

I never set out to become an Agile expert, I kind of stumbled into it. My career began in project management, and like many professionals in that space, I was focused on execution, timelines, and deliverables. But early in my journey, I found myself at a company that was undergoing an Agile transformation. I didn't know it at the time, but that moment would change the trajectory of my career.

As I worked through the transformation, I realized that leading in Agile was fundamentally different from the leadership models I had been taught. Traditional, top-down, command-and-control leadership structures simply didn't work in Agile environments. Instead, leadership had to be built on something deeper, trust, empathy, and empowerment. Agile wasn't just about processes and frameworks, it was a mindset shift that required leaders to show up differently.

This realization led me to pursue my doctorate in leadership, where I focused my dissertation on Agile transformation. The research was eye-opening, it validated much of what I had experienced firsthand while also introducing new perspectives on what makes Agile leadership truly effective. But there was a problem, dissertations aren't exactly light reading.

That's why I wrote this book.

I wanted to take the core insights from my research and make them accessible, practical, and actionable for anyone leading in an Agile world. Whether you are a leader navigating an Agile transformation, an Agile practitioner looking to strengthen your leadership skills, a new or aspiring leader searching for a modern leadership framework, or someone who simply wants to understand what makes great leadership work in today's fast-moving, complex environments, this book is for you.

Inside, you'll find a new way to look at leadership, one that goes beyond methodologies and frameworks. The trust, empathy, and empowerment philosophy serves as a foundation for creating Agile organizations that don't just survive change, but thrive because of it.

Agile leadership isn't just about adapting to change, it's about leading through change in a way that builds strong teams, fosters innovation, and drives long-term success. My hope is that this book challenges your thinking, expands your leadership toolkit, and empowers you to lead with clarity, confidence, and purpose.

Let's get started.

Dr. Kevin Duffy

Author, Agile Leadership: Mastering Trust, Empathy, and Empowerment.

Foreword

In every great leader's journey, there comes a defining moment, a realization that leadership is not about control or titles, but about the people you inspire and the culture you cultivate. My brother, Dr. Kevin Duffy, has captured this essence in *Agile Leadership: Mastering Trust, Empathy, and Empowerment for Organizational Success*. His work is a reflection of years of dedication, resilience, and an unyielding belief in the transformative power of people-first leadership.

Kevin's TEE philosophy—Trust, Empathy, and Empowerment—resonates deeply with me, not just as his brother, but as a fellow leader navigating the evolving landscapes of modern organizations. These principles aren't just theoretical concepts; they are the foundation upon which Kevin has built his career and influenced countless teams. Whether guiding digital delivery at Invesco US or mentoring future leaders, Kevin's approach to Agile leadership is both practical and profoundly human.

What sets this book apart is Kevin's ability to intertwine personal stories with actionable insights. He doesn't just tell you *what* great leadership looks like, he shows you *how* to live it. His commitment to fostering environments where trust flourishes, empathy drives connection, and empowerment sparks innovation is evident on every page.

Having led organizations through growth, transformation, and challenges myself, I can attest to the power of these principles. But Kevin brings clarity and depth to Agile leadership that is rare. He understands that agility isn't just about methodologies, it's about mindset. It's about cultivating a culture where individuals feel seen, heard, and valued, where teams are encouraged to take risks, learn from failures, and celebrate successes together.

Reading this book, you'll find yourself not just learning, but reflecting, on your own leadership style, your impact on others, and your capacity to foster change. Kevin's words will challenge you to lead with authenticity, to embrace vulnerability, and to recognize that the greatest leaders are those who lift others up.

To Kevin: Your dedication to redefining leadership through the lens of trust, empathy, and empowerment is inspiring. This book is not just a contribution to Agile methodologies; it's a roadmap for creating organizations where people thrive. I'm proud to stand alongside you in this journey, and I know that *Agile Leadership* will leave a lasting mark on leaders everywhere.

Dr. Sean R. Duffy

Author of *Leading From Within: The Path to Transformational Leadership*

Chief Operating Officer (COO), MOXFIVE

Introduction: The Need for Agile Leadership

In today's fast-paced world, where entire industries can be disrupted overnight, many leaders find themselves struggling to keep up. As markets evolve, customer preferences shift, and technology accelerates, the old ways of leading simply don't work anymore. Traditional leadership methods, with their rigid hierarchies and top-down decision-making, feel like trying to navigate a storm with an outdated map. It's no wonder leaders often feel lost before they even begin. The question is no longer if change will come, but how leaders can transform their approach to not just survive but thrive in this era of constant flux.

Agile leadership provides a powerful answer. It's not just a buzzword or a strategy confined to tech companies—it's a mindset. Agile leadership is about embracing adaptability, fostering collaboration, and building resilience. But adopting this approach means letting go of old habits and embracing a new way of seeing leadership itself. It requires leaders to shift from controlling every detail to empowering their teams, from sticking to rigid plans to welcoming flexibility and innovation.

The concept of agility has moved far beyond software teams. While the term "agile" may have its roots in the tech industry, its principles have touched every sector—from healthcare and finance to manufacturing and education. At its heart, agility is about being able to pivot quickly in response to change, continuously improving while keeping the customer at the center of every decision. In today's unpredictable markets, this kind of agility isn't just an advantage; it's essential for staying competitive.

Think about how quickly consumer expectations have evolved. Not long ago, customers were content with longer lead times and limited options. Now, they demand personalized, on-demand solutions—and they want them immediately. Digital platforms, social media, and globalized economies have empowered consumers in unprecedented ways. In this environment, organizations that cling to outdated leadership strategies—like rigid hierarchies and command-and-control models—find themselves stuck. Agile leaders, on the other hand, see uncertainty as an opportunity for innovation and growth.

In an agile environment, speed, collaboration, and adaptability become the cornerstones of success. This shift challenges leaders to adopt a new mindset—one that values empowerment over control and flexibility over predictability. Agile leadership isn't just a different style; it's a survival skill in today's dynamic business landscape.

As organizations move toward agile frameworks, leadership becomes the critical factor that can either drive success or derail it. In traditional setups, leaders often act as the primary decision-makers, directing teams from the top down and ensuring every task fits neatly into a pre-defined plan. But agile doesn't operate that way. It's messy, it's fluid, and for many leaders, it's downright uncomfortable.

Agile leadership requires letting go of control, and that can be one of the hardest adjustments to make. In agile organizations, the focus shifts from micromanaging tasks to empowering teams. Leaders don't need to have all the answers anymore. Instead, they need to create environments where teams are trusted to collaborate, experiment, and adapt to change on their own. This transformation from being a "commander" to becoming an "enabler" is at the heart of agile leadership—and it turns traditional leadership norms on their heads.

Consider the common pitfall of micromanagement. Leaders accustomed to overseeing every detail often struggle to trust their teams to take ownership. The result? Bottlenecks, slow decision-making, and frustrated employees. In agile environments, this doesn't just slow things down; it undermines the entire system. Agile teams thrive on autonomy and speed, and when leaders don't step back, they prevent their teams from responding quickly and innovating effectively.

Transparency is another crucial element. Agile teams work in short cycles, constantly adjusting their plans based on feedback from customers and stakeholders. This requires leaders to embrace openness and vulnerability—sharing real-time updates, admitting when things aren't going as planned, and being flexible enough to change course when needed. For many leaders, this level of transparency feels risky. But in agile environments, it's not just encouraged; it's essential.

And then there's adaptability. Agile leadership means leading without a script. Leaders must be comfortable making decisions amidst uncertainty and must encourage their teams to take risks and learn from failures. Instead of setting a rigid path, agile leaders guide their teams toward shared goals, knowing that the route to success will likely shift along the way.

So how do leaders make this shift in mindset? That's where the TEE philosophy comes in—a framework designed to help leaders embrace the core principles of Trust, Empathy, and Empowerment. By focusing on these foundational elements, leaders can not only navigate the challenges of agile transformation but also inspire their teams to thrive in an ever-changing world.

TEE Philosophy

The TEE Philosophy—Trust, Empathy, and Empowerment—provides a clear framework for agile leadership, one that helps navigate the challenges of leading in fast-paced, constantly evolving environments.

Trust: In a traditional setup, trust is often hierarchical—team members trust their leaders to make decisions, and leaders trust the processes they've set up. Agile flips this dynamic. Here, trust is decentralized. Leaders must place trust in their teams, allowing them the freedom to experiment, fail, and learn without micromanagement. In return, teams build confidence and take ownership of their work, which is essential for delivering innovative solutions quickly.

Take, for example, a company undergoing an agile transformation. Leaders who trust their teams to self-organize and manage their own tasks often find that these teams not only meet expectations but exceed them by discovering faster, more efficient ways to solve problems. Trust doesn't just create better results—it strengthens team cohesion and morale, as employees feel valued and empowered.

Empathy: Agile leaders understand that their success is tied to their team's well-being. Empathy is more than just understanding; it's actively listening and responding to the needs of the team. Leaders who practice empathy foster environments where teams feel safe to share their ideas, voice concerns, and seek help when needed. Agile environments thrive when leaders are in tune with their teams, constantly removing roadblocks and providing support.

Imagine a leader who listens carefully to a team's frustrations about an overly complex process. Instead of dismissing these concerns, an empathetic leader acts on them, simplifying the process and clearing the path for productivity. This not only boosts morale but also creates a more agile organization, where employees feel heard and valued.

Empowerment: True empowerment in agile environments goes beyond delegation. It's about giving teams the authority to make decisions, experiment, and adapt. Empowered teams are not waiting for approval—they're actively seeking the best solutions and implementing them swiftly. For leaders, this means stepping back and providing teams with the resources and support they need to succeed.

In many agile success stories, empowerment has been the driving force. For example, a cross-functional team, given the freedom to explore new customer engagement strategies, may develop a breakthrough product feature far quicker than if they had been restricted by a traditional approval hierarchy. Empowered teams drive innovation.

Together, **Trust**, **Empathy**, and **Empowerment** create the environment necessary for agile transformation. Agile leaders who embrace these principles enable their teams to thrive in uncertainty, drive continuous improvement, and build resilient organizations.

Leadership today isn't what it used to be. Gone are the days when a rigid hierarchy and top-down directives were the gold standard. In an era defined by rapid change, technological innovation, and evolving workplace dynamics, the traditional playbook just doesn't cut it anymore. To thrive, leaders must embrace agility—the ability to adapt, pivot, and evolve while fostering an environment where teams can do the same.

Agile leadership isn't just a buzzword or a fleeting trend. It's a transformative approach that redefines how we lead, collaborate, and drive results. At its core, agile leadership is about trust, empathy, and empowerment—the TEE Philosophy. It's about building connections with your team, understanding their unique strengths and challenges, and giving them the autonomy to innovate and excel. This isn't about relinquishing control; it's about creating a culture where control is shared, and leadership is distributed. When leaders trust their teams, show genuine empathy, and empower individuals to take ownership, the results are nothing short of remarkable.

Imagine a workplace where your ideas aren't just heard but valued. Picture a team dynamic where collaboration is the norm, not the exception, and where mistakes are seen as opportunities for growth rather than failures to be punished. This is the essence of agile leadership. It's about shifting from a mindset of command and control to one of inspire and enable. When leaders embody this philosophy, they create a ripple effect, fostering a culture of innovation, resilience, and continuous improvement.

But this transformation doesn't happen overnight. It requires intentional effort, a willingness to challenge old habits, and a commitment to personal growth. Agile leaders are lifelong learners, constantly seeking feedback, reflecting on their experiences, and striving to improve—not just for their own sake, but for the benefit of their teams and organizations. They understand that leadership isn't a destination; it's a journey marked by continuous evolution.

As you dive into the pages ahead, you'll see how the principles of agile leadership—grounded in the TEE Philosophy—can reshape your organization. Whether you're leading a small team or driving transformation at a global scale, agile leadership is your key to unlocking speed, innovation, and adaptability. Embrace the journey, challenge the status quo, and watch as you and your team reach new heights together.

CHAPTER 1

What is Agile?

"The measure of intelligence is the ability to change."
— Albert Einstein

Introduction to Agile

In a world where change is constant, agility has become a necessity, not just a choice. Agile is often associated with software development, but its principles stretch far beyond that. It's a mindset, a philosophy that can be applied to almost any industry—whether you're managing a tech startup, leading a healthcare team, or overseeing a corporate finance department.

At its core, agile is about responding quickly and effectively to change. Traditional business models rely on rigid plans and structured hierarchies, but these frameworks often crumble under the weight of disruption. Agile, on the other hand, thrives in environments where unpredictability is the norm. It encourages flexibility, collaboration, and a focus on delivering value continuously, rather than waiting for perfection.

Agile's ability to adapt in real time makes it an essential tool for leaders looking to stay competitive. Whether it's customer preferences, market trends, or internal processes, those who lead with an agile mindset are better equipped to handle the unknown. They aren't locked into outdated plans; they're able to pivot, reimagine, and innovate in ways that traditional leadership models simply can't match.

The Agile Mindset

The heart of agile lies in its mindset—an approach to work that emphasizes flexibility, continuous improvement, and collaboration. It's not just a set of processes or tools; it's a way of thinking that guides every decision and action within an organization. The agile mindset requires leaders to embrace change, view challenges as opportunities, and focus relentlessly on delivering value.

The **Agile Manifesto**, created in 2001, provides a simple yet powerful framework for this mindset. It's based on four key values:

1. **Individuals and interactions over processes and tools**: Agile prioritizes people—empowered teams and strong collaboration matter more than rigid systems or standardized procedures.

2. **Working solutions over comprehensive documentation**: Instead of getting bogged down in endless planning or documentation, agile focuses on delivering functional results quickly.

3. **Customer collaboration over contract negotiation**: Agile promotes constant communication with customers or stakeholders, ensuring their feedback is integrated at every stage of development.

4. **Responding to change over following a plan**: Agile assumes that change is inevitable. Rather than sticking to a fixed, outdated plan, agile leaders adapt their strategies as new information arises.

But the agile mindset goes beyond these principles—it embraces the idea that learning and improvement are continuous processes. It challenges the traditional top-down leadership structure, where leaders make decisions and employees follow orders. In an agile environment, leadership is decentralized, and decision-making power is often distributed to the teams closest to the work. This empowers employees, speeds up decision-making, and encourages creative problem-solving.

For many organizations, this shift can be uncomfortable at first. Leaders accustomed to hierarchical control may find it difficult to relinquish authority, and employees used to waiting for direction may hesitate to take initiative. However, the agile mindset teaches us that by fostering trust, collaboration, and autonomy, we can unlock higher levels of performance and innovation.

Agile in Action

Agile isn't just a theory—it's a practical, adaptable approach that has transformed industries. From tech startups to global enterprises, agile is being used to innovate, solve complex problems, and deliver value more quickly. To truly understand the impact of agile, it helps to see it in action across different sectors.

Agile in Product Development

One of the most well-known applications of agile is in product development, especially in the tech industry. Take, for example, a software company developing a new app. Rather than spending months planning every feature in detail before any code is written, the team works in **sprints**—short, focused work periods, typically lasting two to four weeks. At the end of each sprint, they deliver a working version of the app, even if it's a basic one. This iterative approach allows the team to gather feedback early, make adjustments, and release improvements with each new sprint.

The key advantage? Flexibility. Instead of waiting until the entire app is finished, the team can adapt based on customer feedback. This minimizes wasted time and resources, ensuring that the final product is exactly what the market needs.

Agile Beyond Tech: Healthcare

Agile principles have found their way into sectors far removed from software. In healthcare, for example, agile methods are being used to improve patient care and operational efficiency. Consider a hospital implementing a new patient management system. Instead of deploying the system all at once across every department, the team applies an agile approach: testing it in one department first, gathering feedback from doctors, nurses, and patients, and then making adjustments before expanding it.

This incremental rollout allows the hospital to catch and fix issues early, improving the final system's effectiveness. More importantly, by involving staff at every step, the hospital fosters a sense of ownership and collaboration, making the transition smoother for everyone involved.

Agile in Finance: Adapting to Market Shifts

The financial sector, known for its structured and risk-averse nature, has also started embracing agile methodologies. Large financial institutions are using agile to stay competitive in an industry that demands rapid adaptation to market trends. For instance, during the implementation of a new digital banking platform, an agile team can release updates to the platform every few weeks instead of waiting for a full-scale launch.

This allows the bank to react quickly to regulatory changes or customer feedback, while also minimizing the risk of rolling out an untested product. In finance, where market conditions can shift suddenly, the ability to adapt quickly offers a competitive edge.

Cross-Sector Agile Practices

Regardless of the industry, agile teams share several core practices that help them function:

- **Daily Standups**: Short, focused team meetings where members discuss what they're working on, any challenges they're facing, and their plans for the day.

- **Iterative Development**: Work is done in small, manageable chunks, allowing for continuous improvement and feedback.

- **Retrospectives**: At the end of each sprint or project phase, teams review what went well, what didn't, and how they can improve in the next cycle.

These agile practices ensure that teams stay aligned, focused, and adaptable, no matter what challenges they face.

The Benefits of Agile

Organizations that embrace agile reap a wide range of benefits, from faster innovation to stronger team collaboration. Agile is more than just a way to manage projects—it's a competitive advantage that helps businesses respond to change quickly and stay ahead of the curve.

Faster Innovation

In traditional project management, teams often spend months or even years developing a product or service before it's launched. Agile flips this model on its head by focusing on delivering smaller, functional versions of the product at regular intervals. This iterative process allows for continuous improvement, as each version can be tested, refined, and enhanced based on feedback.

The result? Innovation happens faster. By delivering working versions early and often, teams can incorporate new ideas, adapt to market demands, and stay ahead of competitors. Agile organizations can respond swiftly to shifts in customer needs or market conditions, giving them the ability to innovate without waiting for a perfect solution.

Improved Collaboration

Agile emphasizes collaboration at every level. Teams are empowered to communicate openly and frequently, ensuring that everyone is aligned on goals and progress. Regular meetings like daily standups, sprint planning, and retrospectives create a culture of transparency and accountability.

This collaborative environment also extends to customers and stakeholders. Agile encourages frequent feedback, so there's no guessing about what the customer wants. Instead, teams work closely with stakeholders throughout the project, adapting their work based on real-time input. This constant collaboration ensures that the final product meets expectations and adds value.

Greater Flexibility

One of the most valuable aspects of agile is its inherent flexibility. In a traditional approach, if a project needs to change direction midway through, it can be costly and time-consuming to pivot. Agile, however, is built to accommodate change.

Teams working in sprints can quickly adjust their focus based on new information or feedback. If a customer changes their requirements, or if market conditions shift, the team can pivot without derailing the entire project. This flexibility reduces risk and allows organizations to remain adaptable in an ever-changing landscape.

Enhanced Customer Satisfaction

At its core, agile is about delivering value to the customer as quickly and efficiently as possible. Instead of waiting for a final product, customers receive working versions throughout the process. This means that they see tangible progress and can offer feedback, ensuring that the final product aligns with their needs.

By involving customers early and often, agile teams can address issues or changes in real-time, leading to higher customer satisfaction. Customers feel heard and valued, and the product or service they receive is more likely to meet—or even exceed—their expectations.

Reduced Waste

Agile's focus on delivering the most valuable features first means that resources are allocated more efficiently. Rather than spending time and money on features that may not be used or appreciated, agile teams focus on what brings the most value to the customer. This reduces wasted time, effort, and resources, leading to a leaner, more efficient operation.

Agile teams regularly review their processes, looking for ways to improve and eliminate unnecessary steps. This constant refinement helps organizations operate more efficiently and effectively, maximizing their return on investment.

Agile Misconceptions

Despite its growing popularity, there are several common misconceptions about agile that can prevent leaders from fully embracing it. These misunderstandings often stem from a narrow or incomplete view of what agile truly is.

Misconception: Agile is Only for Tech Teams

One of the most pervasive myths is that agile is only relevant for software development or tech-focused teams. While agile did originate in the world of software, its principles—like flexibility, collaboration, and iterative progress—can be applied across all sectors. Whether you're in marketing, finance, healthcare, or manufacturing, agile offers a framework for tackling complex problems and adapting to change.

Agile's core values are universally applicable: focusing on people, responding to change, and delivering value early and often. Any team that faces uncertainty, evolving demands, or needs to improve collaboration can benefit from an agile approach.

Misconception: Agile Means No Structure

Some people believe that adopting agile means abandoning structure altogether, leading to chaos. In reality, agile frameworks, like Scrum or Kanban, provide clear structures and processes for how teams work together. These structures create an environment that encourages frequent feedback, incremental progress, and accountability.

Agile doesn't eliminate planning—it just changes the approach. Instead of rigid, long-term plans, agile relies on shorter cycles of planning, development, and feedback. This allows teams to adapt as they learn, without losing sight of their larger goals.

Misconception: Agile is Faster, But Sloppier

Another misconception is that agile is about speed at the cost of quality. While agile does promote faster delivery, the emphasis is on delivering value incrementally, not rushing to meet deadlines. Agile teams continuously refine their work, incorporating feedback to ensure high-quality results.

The iterative nature of agile allows teams to catch mistakes earlier, reducing the risk of large-scale project failures. Instead of scrambling to fix a massive issue at the end of a project, agile teams identify and resolve problems in real-time, leading to more robust and reliable outcomes.

Misconception: Agile is Only for Small Teams

Some believe that agile only works for small, nimble teams. However, agile principles can be scaled to fit larger organizations. Frameworks like **Scaled Agile Framework (SAFe)** have been developed to help large enterprises implement agile practices across multiple teams and departments.

In fact, large organizations that adopt agile often see more dramatic improvements in collaboration, innovation, and adaptability, precisely because agile helps break down silos and encourage cross-functional teamwork.

Closing Thoughts

Agile isn't just a set of processes; it's a philosophy that challenges the way we think about leadership, teamwork, and innovation. By embracing the agile mindset, organizations can become more responsive to change, more focused on delivering value, and better equipped to handle the unknown.

As we continue through this book, we'll explore how agile principles can be applied to leadership, not just in theory but in practical, everyday scenarios. Agile leadership is about empowering teams, fostering trust, and creating environments where continuous improvement becomes second nature.

Next, we'll take a closer look at one of the biggest hurdles leaders face when adopting agile—understanding why traditional leadership models often struggle in agile environments.

Case Study: Sipgate – German Telecommunications

Overview:

Sipgate, a German telecommunications company, faced significant challenges prior to 2010, including interdepartmental conflicts, slow product development cycles, and a rigid management structure that stifled innovation. To address these issues, Sipgate adopted Scrum and Lean methodologies, marking a transformative shift towards Agile practices. This decision was driven by the need for greater flexibility, improved collaboration, and faster product delivery.

The transformation process at Sipgate included:

- Empowering Cross-Functional Teams: Teams were restructured to be cross-functional and self-organizing, breaking down silos and encouraging collaboration between departments. This shift helped reduce interdepartmental conflicts and improved communication.

- Adopting Lean Principles: By embracing Lean, Sipgate focused on eliminating waste, optimizing processes, and delivering customer value more efficiently. Lean thinking helped streamline workflows and enhance productivity.

- Transparency and Continuous Feedback: The introduction of daily stand-ups, sprint reviews, and retrospectives created a culture of openness and continuous feedback. Teams could quickly identify bottlenecks, address issues, and adapt to changes.

- Leadership Transformation: Management shifted from a command-and-control style to a servant leadership approach, fostering trust and empowering teams to make decisions. Leaders supported the teams by removing obstacles and providing the resources needed for success.

Challenges Faced:

Sipgate's transformation was not without hurdles. The shift to Agile required a fundamental change in mindset, which initially met resistance. Teams had to learn to trust the new processes, and management had to relinquish control in favor of empowerment. Through consistent coaching, training, and a commitment to the Agile principles, these challenges were gradually overcome.

Outcome:

The Agile transformation at Sipgate delivered impressive results:

- Improved Cohesion: Cross-functional teams worked together more effectively, leading to a significant reduction in interdepartmental conflicts.

- Faster Product Delivery: Development cycles were shortened, allowing Sipgate to deliver new products and features at a much faster pace, keeping them competitive in the market.

- Cultural Shift: The adoption of Agile fostered a culture of continuous improvement, where teams were encouraged to experiment, learn, and evolve. This mindset shift created an environment where innovation thrived.

- Higher Transparency: Enhanced communication and transparency across teams led to better alignment and a clearer understanding of goals and priorities.

Sipgate's experience highlights the transformative power of Agile and Lean principles in overcoming organizational challenges and driving meaningful change.

Key Takeaway:

Sipgate's journey demonstrates that by embracing Agile methodologies, companies can resolve long-standing challenges, improve collaboration, and create a culture of continuous improvement. Trust, empathy, and empowerment were critical elements in achieving these outcomes, aligning perfectly with the TEE Philosophy.

Why: The Wright Brothers' innovation and iterative approach to achieving powered flight is a perfect historical analogy for the agile process of trial, adaptation, and success. Their method of learning from each test flight mirrors the core principles of agile methodology.

CHAPTER 2

Why Leaders Struggle with Agile

"Leadership is not about being in charge. It's about taking care of those in your charge."
— Simon Sinek

Introduction

Agile has proven itself as a powerful approach for driving innovation and adaptability. Yet, many leaders who understand the value of agile still struggle to put its principles into practice. It's not because they lack the knowledge or motivation, but because agile requires a fundamental shift in how leadership is understood and exercised. Leaders who have spent years perfecting their ability to control outcomes, make decisions, and manage top-down often find it difficult to adapt to agile's demands for trust, collaboration, and flexibility.

This struggle is not unique. In fact, it's one of the most common roadblocks organizations face during agile transformations. At its core, agile challenges traditional leadership models, forcing leaders to question the very strategies that once made them successful. To lead effectively in an agile environment, leaders must let go of deeply ingrained habits and embrace new ways of thinking. For many, this is the hardest part of the journey.

The Leadership Paradigm Shift

Traditional leadership is built on a foundation of control. Leaders, often positioned at the top of a hierarchical structure, make decisions, set goals, and delegate tasks to their teams. The focus is on efficiency, predictability, and maintaining order. In this model, success is measured by how well teams execute the leader's vision, with little room for deviation.

Agile, however, turns this model on its head. Agile leadership is about facilitating rather than controlling—leaders are no longer the sole decision-makers, but rather enablers who create environments where teams can thrive. This shift requires a change in mindset, from seeing leadership as "directing" to viewing it as "supporting."

For leaders accustomed to being in charge, this can feel like a loss of power. Instead of having all the answers, agile leaders need to trust their teams to experiment, make mistakes, and ultimately find the best path forward. This decentralization of decision-making can be uncomfortable, especially when leaders are used to providing clear direction and seeing it followed precisely.

The challenge for many leaders lies in the unpredictability of agile. Unlike traditional methods where a plan is laid out and followed step by step, agile embraces uncertainty. Teams iterate, learn, and pivot based on feedback, which can seem chaotic to leaders accustomed to sticking to a plan. The reality, however, is that this flexibility leads to better results in environments where customer needs and market conditions are constantly changing.

Agile leaders must also shift their focus from individual performance to team collaboration. In traditional settings, leaders often reward individual achievements, but agile prioritizes the collective success of the team. This requires a new way of motivating and supporting teams—one that emphasizes trust, collaboration, and shared goals rather than individual competition.

Control vs. Trust

One of the biggest hurdles for leaders transitioning to agile is the shift from control to trust. In traditional leadership models, leaders maintain tight control over decisions, timelines, and deliverables. This hands-on approach often comes from a desire to ensure that everything runs smoothly and that the organization meets its goals. But in an agile environment, such control is not only impractical—it's counterproductive.

Agile thrives on team autonomy. Teams are expected to make decisions quickly, adapt to new information, and find solutions without waiting for approval from the top. This level of empowerment is essential for agile to work, but it can feel like a leap of faith for leaders who are used to being in control of every detail.

The reality is that trust, not control, is the foundation of agile leadership. Leaders must trust that their teams have the skills, knowledge, and motivation to deliver results. This doesn't mean abandoning accountability—it means shifting it. Rather than micromanaging tasks, agile leaders focus on outcomes. They set the vision, provide the necessary resources, and then trust their teams to find the best way to achieve the goals.

Trust is built gradually. Leaders who struggle with letting go of control can start by giving teams more ownership over smaller decisions. Over time, as teams prove their capability, leaders can step back even further, providing guidance only when needed. The more trust a leader places in their team, the more the team rises to meet expectations, creating a cycle of mutual respect and confidence.

Transparency and Vulnerability

Transparency and vulnerability are two traits not often associated with traditional leadership. In many corporate environments, leaders feel pressure to appear infallible, always knowing the right answers and having a clear path forward. But in agile environments, this need for control and certainty is not just unnecessary—it can be harmful.

Agile teams thrive on open communication and transparency. Leaders must be willing to share both successes and failures openly with their teams. This includes admitting when things aren't going as planned and being open to changing direction. In an agile environment, leaders don't hide mistakes or try to manage perception. Instead, they foster a culture of learning by being upfront about challenges and encouraging their teams to do the same.

This kind of transparency builds trust and strengthens collaboration. When leaders are open about what's working and what isn't, it creates a safe environment where team members feel comfortable sharing their own challenges. It breaks down the fear of failure and encourages continuous improvement, a core tenet of agile.

Being transparent also means being vulnerable. Leaders must be comfortable admitting when they don't have all the answers, especially in uncertain situations. This doesn't undermine a leader's authority; it humanizes them. In agile, vulnerability is a strength because it encourages teams to step up and contribute their insights and expertise. It fosters a culture of collective problem-solving, where leadership is shared, and everyone has a stake in the outcome.

The Fear of Failure

For many leaders, the fear of failure is a significant obstacle in adopting agile practices. In traditional environments, failure is often seen as a weakness—something to be avoided at all costs. Leaders feel the pressure to deliver results without mistakes, and this mindset trickles down to their teams, creating a culture where risks are minimized, and innovation is stifled.

In agile, however, failure is not just accepted—it's embraced as a key part of the learning process. The concept of "failing fast" is central to agile methodology. Teams are encouraged to experiment, try new approaches, and learn from their mistakes quickly, before moving on to the next iteration. This allows for continuous improvement and innovation, but it requires leaders to be comfortable with the idea that not every initiative will succeed on the first try.

The challenge for many leaders is reframing their relationship with failure. Instead of viewing it as a reflection of incompetence, agile leaders see failure as a learning opportunity. When teams are allowed to take risks and make mistakes, they uncover valuable insights that can lead to breakthroughs in performance and creativity.

Leaders must also create a culture where failure is safe—where team members know that their mistakes won't be met with blame or punishment, but with constructive feedback and support. This shift in mindset encourages teams to push boundaries, try new things, and ultimately deliver more innovative solutions.

For leaders who have built their careers on avoiding failure, this can be a difficult adjustment. However, by fostering an environment where teams are free to fail fast, learn, and adapt, leaders can unlock the true potential of agile

Closing Thoughts

Adopting an agile mindset isn't just about learning new processes—it's about reshaping how leaders think about control, trust, transparency, and failure. The struggles leaders face when transitioning to agile are often rooted in the habits and strategies that once made them successful in traditional environments. But as the business landscape evolves, so too must leadership.

In the chapters ahead, we'll explore how leaders can overcome these challenges by embracing the principles of the TEE philosophy—Trust, Empathy, and Empowerment. By integrating these values into their leadership approach, leaders can create the conditions for agile to thrive.

Case Study: John Deere

Overview: John Deere, a global leader in agricultural and construction machinery manufacturing, recognized the need for greater efficiency, adaptability, and customer-focused innovation. To achieve this, the company embarked on an ambitious journey to implement Agile practices at scale within its IT teams. Leveraging the Scrum@Scale framework, John Deere sought to transform not just individual teams but entire departments, creating a more responsive and collaborative organizational culture. This large-scale transformation engaged over 2,500 employees and spanned multiple regions and functional areas.

The transformation process involved:

- Structured Wave/Phase Training: Teams were trained in structured phases, allowing them to gradually adopt Agile practices while minimizing disruption to ongoing projects. This phased approach ensured that learning was incremental and continuously reinforced.

- Continuous Coaching and Support: John Deere invested in dedicated Agile coaches who worked closely with teams to guide them through the transition. Leadership actively supported the change, reinforcing a culture of trust and continuous improvement.

- Alignment and Transparency: Using the Scrum@Scale framework allowed John Deere to align teams towards common goals while maintaining transparency across multiple levels of the organization. Regular Scrum of Scrums meetings facilitated communication and coordination between teams, ensuring obstacles were identified and addressed promptly.

Challenges Faced: Like any large-scale transformation, John Deere encountered challenges, including resistance to change, the complexity of scaling Agile principles, and the need to balance ongoing delivery with transformation efforts. Through open communication, leadership commitment, and iterative improvements, the company navigated these challenges effectively.

Outcome: The results of John Deere's Agile transformation were substantial:

- Improved Team Performance: Teams reported higher levels of productivity, efficiency, and collaboration.
- Faster Product Delivery: The time to deliver new features and updates was significantly reduced, enabling John Deere to respond more quickly to customer needs and market demands.
- Enhanced Employee Engagement: Employees experienced increased ownership, satisfaction, and morale due to clearer roles, better communication, and a sense of empowerment.
- Sustained Agility: The continuous coaching model helped John Deere sustain its Agile practices, embedding a culture of continuous learning and adaptation.

John Deere's success demonstrates that large-scale Agile transformations are achievable with the right combination of structured training, leadership support, and a commitment to the core principles of trust, empathy, and empowerment.

Key Takeaway: John Deere's journey exemplifies how embracing Agile at scale can lead to measurable improvements in performance, delivery, and culture, reinforcing the power of the TEE Philosophy in driving successful transformations.

Why: Lincoln faced immense resistance while trying to lead during one of the most challenging periods in U.S. history. His perseverance and ability to adapt align with the struggles leaders face when implementing transformative change, including agile practices.

CHAPTER 3

Servant Leadership

"The first responsibility of a leader is to define reality. The last is to say thank you. In between, the leader is a servant."
— Max De Pree

Introduction

At the heart of agile leadership lies an approach that flips traditional leadership on its head: servant leadership. Unlike the command-and-control models that place leaders at the top, directing and overseeing their teams, servant leadership is about placing the needs of the team first. Servant leaders are not the ones giving orders from above; they are the ones lifting their teams up, enabling them to perform at their best.

In agile environments, this leadership style is essential. Agile thrives on collaboration, trust, and empowerment—values that are central to servant leadership. Instead of focusing on personal power or authority, servant leaders focus on helping their teams succeed. They serve as enablers, creating the conditions where teams can innovate, solve problems, and grow. This shift from controlling to serving is one of the most powerful tools a leader can use in an agile transformation.

The Core Traits of Servant Leadership

Empathy One of the most defining traits of a servant leader is empathy. Servant leaders take the time to understand the needs, challenges, and aspirations of their team members. This deep understanding allows them to support their teams in meaningful ways—whether that's providing resources, removing roadblocks, or simply offering emotional support.

In agile environments, empathy is especially crucial. Agile teams rely on strong collaboration, and a leader who shows empathy fosters a culture of trust and openness. When leaders genuinely care about their team members, it builds loyalty and encourages everyone to contribute their best ideas and efforts.

Listening Servant leaders don't just lead—they listen. They actively seek feedback from their teams, encouraging open dialogue and valuing the perspectives of others. In a traditional leadership model, decisions often flow top-down, with little input from the team. But in agile, servant leaders understand that the best ideas often come from the people closest to the work.

By listening to their teams, servant leaders can make more informed decisions and create a sense of ownership among team members. Listening also helps leaders identify issues early and adjust strategies based on real-time feedback, aligning with agile's iterative approach.

Humility True servant leaders lead with humility. They recognize that their role is not to be the hero of the story but to empower their teams to succeed. This means setting aside ego and focusing on the collective success of the team, rather than personal accolades.

In an agile context, humility allows leaders to delegate responsibility, trust their teams to make decisions, and accept that they don't always have all the answers. Humble leaders create a space where team members feel valued and empowered, leading to higher levels of engagement and innovation.

Stewardship Servant leaders view themselves as stewards, entrusted with the care of their teams, resources, and the broader organization. Stewardship goes beyond managing—it's about taking responsibility for the well-being and growth of the people and the organization they serve. Agile leaders act as stewards by guiding their teams toward success, while also protecting the long-term health of the organization.

In practice, this means servant leaders are committed to ethical decision-making, sustainable growth, and creating a positive culture that fosters both personal and professional development. They take care of the "bigger picture" while ensuring their teams have what they need to succeed on a day-to-day basis.

Empowering Teams

One of the most powerful ways servant leaders contribute to agile environments is by empowering their teams. In traditional settings, leaders often maintain control, directing every decision and managing tasks closely. In contrast, servant leaders understand that true empowerment comes from granting their teams the autonomy to make decisions, solve problems, and take ownership of their work.

Empowering teams isn't about handing over responsibilities and stepping back; it's about creating the conditions for success. Servant leaders provide their teams with the tools, resources, and support they need to thrive. They build trust by showing confidence in their teams' abilities, which encourages team members to take initiative, experiment, and innovate without fear of micromanagement.

In an agile environment, this empowerment is critical. Agile teams must be able to pivot quickly, make decisions in real-time, and respond to changes without waiting for approval from above. When leaders empower their teams, they unlock the full potential of agile by allowing teams to operate with speed and creativity. The result is a more dynamic, engaged, and productive team, capable of delivering high-quality results faster and with greater ownership of the process.

Collaboration and Growth

Servant leaders foster an environment where collaboration and growth are central to team dynamics. Agile thrives on teamwork—where cross-functional teams work together to solve problems, develop solutions, and continuously improve. Servant leadership amplifies this by encouraging open communication, mutual respect, and shared responsibility.

Collaboration in agile isn't just about working together; it's about creating a culture where everyone feels valued and heard. Servant leaders promote this by encouraging team members to share their ideas, provide feedback, and contribute to the decision-making process. By removing barriers and promoting a culture of openness, servant leaders help teams become more cohesive and effective.

In addition to promoting collaboration, servant leaders are deeply committed to the growth and development of their team members. They view leadership as an opportunity to mentor and coach, helping individuals grow both professionally and personally. Whether through formal training, offering new challenges, or simply providing regular feedback, servant leaders invest in their teams' development.

In an agile environment, this focus on growth ensures that teams are continuously learning and improving. As teams grow, they become more adaptable, resilient, and capable of handling the challenges of an ever-changing business landscape. Servant leaders understand that by investing in the growth of their people, they are also investing in the long-term success of the organization.

Servant Leadership in Action

To see the true impact of servant leadership in an agile environment, it helps to look at real-world examples where this leadership style has transformed teams and organizations. One powerful example comes from the tech industry, where agile methodologies are often coupled with servant leadership principles to drive innovation.

Consider the case of a global tech company that was struggling with slow product development cycles. The traditional leadership model wasn't working—decisions took too long, and teams felt disconnected from the company's vision. After adopting servant leadership principles, the company saw a dramatic shift. Leaders began focusing on serving their teams, removing obstacles, and empowering them to take ownership of their projects. Teams were encouraged to experiment, fail fast, and iterate on their ideas.

The results were remarkable. Product development cycles sped up, collaboration improved, and employee morale soared. Teams felt more engaged and motivated because they were trusted to lead their own work. This transformation wasn't just about adopting agile practices—it was about shifting leadership from control to service.

Another example comes from healthcare, where servant leadership has been used to foster collaboration in cross-functional teams. In one hospital, leaders worked closely with doctors, nurses, and administrative staff to identify barriers to patient care. By listening and empowering the teams to implement their own solutions, the hospital saw significant improvements in patient outcomes. The leadership team's role shifted from directing operations to supporting the frontline workers, allowing those closest to the work to lead the change.

These examples illustrate the power of servant leadership in agile environments. By focusing on trust, collaboration, and empowerment, servant leaders create a culture where teams can thrive, adapt, and innovate.

Closing Thoughts

Servant leadership is the cornerstone of agile success. By putting the needs of the team first, empowering individuals, and fostering a culture of collaboration and growth, servant leaders unlock the full potential of their teams. In the fast-paced, ever-changing world of agile, this approach is not only effective—it's essential.

As we move forward, we'll explore the practical steps leaders can take to develop servant leadership traits and apply them in their organizations. By adopting the principles of Trust, Empathy, and Empowerment, leaders can create agile teams that are resilient, innovative, and capable of driving lasting transformation.

Case Study: Valpak

Overview:

Valpak, a leading direct marketing company known for its coupon mailers and digital promotions, faced challenges with slow product development, siloed departments, and a need for greater efficiency in its workflows. Recognizing the need for a fundamental shift, Valpak adopted the **Scaled Agile Framework (SAFe)** to drive its Agile transformation. The company understood that successful transformation required both **top-down leadership support** and **bottom-up team engagement** to foster a culture of trust, collaboration, and empowerment.

The transformation process involved:

- **Integrating Scrum and Kanban:** Valpak implemented **Scrum** for iterative development and **Kanban** for managing continuous workflows. This dual approach allowed teams to choose the methodology that best suited their type of work, ensuring flexibility and efficiency.
- **Leadership Engagement:** Leaders at Valpak played an active role in supporting Agile practices, removing impediments, and

promoting a culture of transparency. This leadership commitment was critical in maintaining momentum and reinforcing the principles of trust and empowerment.
- **Team Collaboration:** By breaking down silos and encouraging cross-functional collaboration, Valpak's teams were better aligned with company goals. Regular ceremonies such as sprint planning, daily stand-ups, and retrospectives fostered open communication and continuous improvement.
- **Wave-Based Training:** Teams adopted Agile practices in phases, allowing for gradual learning and adaptation. This approach reduced disruption and helped embed Agile principles more effectively.

Challenges Faced:

The transition to Agile required a shift in mindset for both leadership and teams. Resistance to change, learning new frameworks, and integrating Scrum and Kanban across different workflows were initial hurdles. However, consistent training, coaching, and leadership support helped overcome these obstacles.

Outcome:

Valpak's Agile transformation resulted in:

- **Improved Team Effectiveness:** Teams became more efficient, productive, and collaborative, delivering higher-quality products more consistently.
- **Faster Product Delivery:** The integration of Scrum and Kanban reduced development cycles, allowing Valpak to bring products to market more quickly and respond to customer needs with agility.

- **Business Results:** The overall business performance improved, with better alignment between teams and organizational objectives. The transformation fostered a culture of trust, transparency, and continuous improvement.
- **Employee Empowerment:** Teams experienced higher levels of ownership, engagement, and satisfaction, contributing to a more dynamic and innovative workplace.

Valpak's journey illustrates that with the right framework, leadership support, and commitment to Agile principles, organizations can achieve significant improvements in efficiency, team performance, and business outcomes.

Key Takeaway:

Valpak's successful adoption of SAFe, Scrum, and Kanban showcases how trust, empathy, and empowerment can drive effective Agile transformations, leading to lasting improvements in both team dynamics and business results.

Why: Gandhi exemplifies servant leadership, where the leader's role is to serve the people. His leadership approach of humility, service, and empowerment reflects the core of servant leadership in both business and life.

CHAPTER 4

Building Agile Teams

"Coming together is a beginning, staying together is progress, and working together is success."
— Henry Ford

Introduction

Agile teams are the engine that drives successful transformations. Unlike traditional teams that rely on top-down direction, agile teams are designed to be flexible, self-organizing, and highly collaborative. They are built to adapt, solve problems, and deliver value quickly, even in uncertain or changing environments. But building an agile team isn't as simple as assembling a group of skilled individuals—it requires a deliberate focus on creating the right dynamics, fostering trust, and aligning everyone around shared goals.

At the core of agile teams is the belief that diverse skills and perspectives, when combined, lead to better decision-making and innovation. Cross-functional teams that can manage everything from development to design to delivery are the backbone of agility. These teams don't wait for instructions—they act, iterate, and improve continuously. In this chapter, we'll explore the key principles behind building agile teams, including cross-functionality, self-organization, and the importance of communication and continuous improvement.

Cross-Functionality and Team Roles

One of the defining features of agile teams is their cross-functional nature. Cross-functional teams are made up of individuals with a wide range of skills, each contributing their expertise to a common goal. Instead of siloing tasks by department or function, agile teams bring together developers, designers, testers, product owners, and other roles to work side by side. This diversity of skills allows the team to handle all aspects of a project, from ideation to execution, without relying on external dependencies.

Cross-functional teams are essential for agility because they can respond to changes quickly and efficiently. When teams have all the skills they need within the group, they can adapt to shifting priorities or customer feedback without waiting for handoffs or approvals from other departments. This speed and flexibility are key to delivering high-quality results in fast-paced environments.

Within agile teams, roles are clearly defined, but they differ from the rigid hierarchies found in traditional organizations. Three key roles form the foundation of most agile teams:

1. **The Product Owner**: The product owner is responsible for representing the voice of the customer. They ensure that the team is working on the most valuable features by prioritizing the product backlog and setting clear goals for the team. The product owner serves as the bridge between the business and the team, continuously gathering feedback and refining the product vision to meet customer needs.

2. **The Scrum Master (or Agile Coach)**: The scrum master acts as a facilitator for the team, ensuring that agile processes are followed and helping to remove any obstacles that could slow down the team's progress. While the scrum master doesn't have formal authority over the team, they play a critical role in coaching the team to self-organize, resolve conflicts, and stay focused on delivering value.

3. **The Development Team**: This group includes all the individuals responsible for creating the product, from developers to designers to testers. Unlike in traditional teams, where roles are often rigidly defined, agile development teams are expected to collaborate and contribute to multiple aspects of the project. This flexibility allows the team to quickly adjust

to changing requirements and deliver functional products in short iterations.

By building cross-functional teams with well-defined roles, organizations can create a structure that supports agility. These teams can move quickly, solve problems collaboratively, and deliver high-value products in shorter time frames.

Self-Organizing Teams

One of the most distinctive characteristics of agile teams is their ability to self-organize. Unlike traditional teams that rely on a manager or leader to direct their tasks and priorities, self-organizing teams take ownership of their work. They are empowered to make decisions, solve problems, and manage their workflow without waiting for top-down direction.

In an agile environment, self-organizing teams are given a clear goal, but how they achieve that goal is left up to them. This autonomy allows teams to adapt quickly to changing requirements, pivot when necessary, and experiment with new approaches. It also fosters a sense of responsibility and accountability within the team, as every member is invested in the outcome.

Self-organization doesn't mean chaos or a lack of structure—it's about creating an environment where the team can operate efficiently without constant oversight. Teams still follow agile processes like sprint planning, daily standups, and retrospectives, but within those frameworks, they have the freedom to decide how best to collaborate and deliver results.

For self-organizing teams to thrive, trust is key. Leaders must trust that their teams are capable of managing their work, and team members must trust one another to fulfill their roles and contribute effectively. This trust is built over time, through transparent communication, shared goals, and a culture of collaboration.

Self-organizing teams are also flexible. Team members often wear multiple hats, contributing to different areas of the project as needed. This cross-functional collaboration ensures that teams are resilient, able to tackle challenges from multiple angles, and adapt to new demands without missing a beat.

Collaboration and Communication

Collaboration is the lifeblood of agile teams. Agile teams work in close-knit units where communication is constant and transparent. This is what allows them to make quick decisions, adapt to changes, and maintain alignment on goals. Effective collaboration helps teams move faster, resolve conflicts early, and ensure that everyone is working toward the same outcomes.

Agile practices like daily standups, sprint reviews, and retrospectives create regular opportunities for team members to share updates, discuss roadblocks, and brainstorm solutions. These meetings keep everyone in the loop and foster a sense of shared responsibility.

- **Daily Standups**: In this short, focused meeting, team members share what they worked on yesterday, what they plan to do today, and any obstacles they're facing. These quick check-ins keep the team aligned and help identify issues before they become bigger problems.
- **Sprint Planning**: At the beginning of each sprint, the team gathers to plan their work. This collaborative session ensures that everyone has a clear understanding of the priorities and goals for the upcoming iteration.

- **Retrospectives**: After each sprint, the team reflects on what went well, what didn't, and how they can improve in the next iteration. This commitment to continuous improvement is a hallmark of agile teams and ensures that the team is always learning and evolving.

Collaboration doesn't just happen in meetings—it's a mindset. Agile teams thrive when communication flows freely, and every member feels empowered to contribute ideas and offer feedback. Servant leaders play a crucial role in fostering this environment by encouraging open dialogue and removing barriers to communication.

In today's world, where teams are often distributed across different locations, tools like Slack, Jira, and Zoom have become essential for maintaining strong communication and collaboration. These tools allow teams to stay connected, even when working remotely, ensuring that agility is not compromised by distance.

Continuous Improvement

Continuous improvement is one of the most important principles of agile. Agile teams are always looking for ways to get better—whether that means improving processes, enhancing collaboration, or delivering higher-quality results. This mindset of constant learning and refinement is what sets agile teams apart, and it's driven by a culture of feedback and reflection.

At the heart of continuous improvement are the regular **retrospectives** that take place at the end of each sprint. In these sessions, the team reflects on what went well, what didn't, and how they can improve moving forward. These conversations aren't about pointing fingers or assigning blame—they're about identifying opportunities for growth and learning from mistakes. The goal is to create a culture where the team feels safe to openly discuss challenges and where solutions can be found collaboratively.

Agile teams also practice **incremental improvement.** Instead of waiting for a major overhaul or redesign, agile teams make small, manageable changes throughout the course of a project. This allows for faster adaptation and ensures that the team is always making progress. By regularly reviewing their processes and outcomes, teams can identify inefficiencies or bottlenecks early and adjust accordingly.

This focus on continuous improvement also extends to personal development. Agile teams are encouraged to invest in their own learning and growth. Whether through formal training, experimenting with new tools, or simply sharing knowledge within the team, individuals are constantly developing new skills that contribute to the overall success of the team.

Ultimately, continuous improvement is about fostering a **growth mindset**—the belief that abilities can be developed and challenges are opportunities for learning. Teams that embrace this mindset are not only more agile but also more resilient, capable of adapting to changes and thriving in the face of uncertainty.

Closing Thoughts

Building agile teams requires more than just assembling a group of talented individuals—it requires creating an environment where collaboration, trust, and continuous improvement are at the forefront. Agile teams are cross-functional, self-organizing, and committed to delivering value in every iteration. They thrive on open communication and are always looking for ways to get better.

As we move forward, we'll explore how to foster a culture of agility within the broader organization. By embedding these principles into the fabric of the company, leaders can ensure that agility is not just limited to teams, but becomes a way of doing business across the entire organization.

Case Study: Penta Technologies

Overview:

Penta Technologies, a software company serving the construction industry, faced challenges stemming from siloed teams, inefficient workflows, and slow delivery times. To address these issues, Penta adopted **Scrum** as part of their Agile transformation. The goal was to break down silos, empower teams, and create a more collaborative and responsive environment for product development.

The transformation process included:

- **Cross-Functional Teams:** Penta restructured their teams to be cross-functional, combining developers, testers, and business analysts into cohesive units. This structure improved communication, reduced bottlenecks, and allowed for more effective collaboration.
- **Adopting Scrum Practices:** By implementing Scrum ceremonies such as sprint planning, daily stand-ups, sprint reviews, and retrospectives, Penta established a regular cadence of work. This iterative approach allowed teams to deliver smaller, valuable increments more frequently.
- **Empowered Decision-Making:** Teams were given greater autonomy to make decisions and solve problems. This empowerment fostered a sense of ownership, accountability, and creativity.

- **Leadership Support:** Penta's leadership actively supported the Agile transformation, promoting a culture of trust and continuous improvement. Leaders focused on enabling teams rather than directing them, reinforcing the principles of servant leadership.
- **Continuous Feedback and Adaptation:** Regular retrospectives provided opportunities for teams to reflect on their processes and make continuous improvements. This feedback loop contributed to ongoing growth and adaptation.

Challenges Faced:

Shifting from a siloed, hierarchical structure to self-organizing Agile teams required a significant change in mindset. Some employees were initially resistant to new processes, and there were challenges in establishing trust and communication between departments. Through consistent coaching, transparent communication, and visible leadership support, these challenges were gradually overcome.

Outcome:

Penta Technologies' Agile transformation delivered remarkable results:

- **Employee Satisfaction:** Employee satisfaction increased dramatically, jumping from **38% to 98%**. Teams felt more engaged, valued, and motivated due to the collaborative and empowering environment.
- **Improved Delivery Times:** The adoption of Scrum practices significantly reduced delivery times, enabling Penta to release software updates and new features faster and more reliably.

- **Collaborative Culture:** Siloed teams were replaced by highly collaborative, cross-functional units. This cultural shift led to better problem-solving, innovation, and overall team cohesion.
- **Sustained Agility:** The continuous feedback and improvement cycle ensured that Penta's Agile practices remained dynamic and responsive to changing needs.

Penta's experience highlights the transformative impact of empowering teams through Agile principles. By embracing trust, empathy, and empowerment, the company fostered a workplace where people thrive, and business outcomes improve.

Key Takeaway:

Penta Technologies' journey demonstrates that breaking down silos, empowering teams, and adopting Scrum practices can lead to remarkable improvements in employee satisfaction, delivery times, and organizational culture. This case underscores the power of trust, empathy, and empowerment in driving successful Agile transformations.

Why: The interdisciplinary team that worked on the Manhattan Project exemplifies how diverse, high-performing teams can collaborate to achieve extraordinary results. The project involved collaboration across various fields, just like agile teams.

CHAPTER 5

Fostering a Culture of Agility

"The only way to do great work is to love what you do."
— Steve Jobs

Introduction

For agile to truly thrive in an organization, it must extend beyond individual teams and become part of the company's culture. While implementing agile practices within isolated teams can lead to short-term improvements, sustainable transformation requires an organizational commitment to agility. This means embedding agile values—like collaboration, adaptability, and continuous improvement—into every level of the company, from leadership to frontline employees.

Fostering a culture of agility isn't about changing processes alone; it's about shifting mindsets. Leaders must champion this change, creating an environment where teams feel empowered to innovate, learn, and adapt. When agility becomes part of the company's DNA, organizations are better equipped to navigate uncertainty, respond to customer needs, and stay ahead in competitive markets.

The Role of Leadership in Cultural Change

Leaders play a critical role in driving cultural change. Without leadership's commitment to fostering agility, even the best agile practices within teams can falter. It's not enough for leaders to mandate agile practices—they must actively participate in and promote agile principles through their actions, decisions, and communication.

Leading by Example: Agile transformation starts at the top. Leaders must model the behaviors they want to see in their teams. This means embracing transparency, showing vulnerability, and demonstrating a willingness to adapt. For example, leaders can hold regular open discussions with teams, sharing challenges and progress openly, rather than keeping information siloed or hierarchical.

When leaders embody agile principles like collaboration and trust, it sets the tone for the rest of the organization. Employees take their cues from leadership, and when they see leaders practicing agility, it reinforces the message that this is the new normal—not just a passing trend.

Promoting Transparency: In agile organizations, transparency is key to building trust and alignment. Leaders must create an environment where information flows freely, allowing teams to make informed decisions. This includes being transparent about business goals, priorities, and even failures. When teams understand the bigger picture, they are better equipped to align their efforts with organizational objectives and make decisions that drive value.

Promoting transparency also means removing barriers that prevent open communication. Leaders should encourage feedback from all levels of the organization and be willing to listen, adapt, and respond to concerns raised by employees.

Supporting Continuous Learning: One of the most important roles of leadership in an agile organization is fostering a culture of continuous learning. Agile thrives on experimentation and iteration, and leaders must encourage their teams to take risks, learn from failures, and improve with each iteration.

This commitment to learning extends beyond teams—it's something that leaders must practice themselves. Leaders who are open to feedback, willing to learn from their mistakes, and eager to experiment set the standard for the rest of the organization. By supporting continuous learning, leaders not only enhance the performance of their teams but also cultivate an agile mindset that permeates the entire organization.

Aligning Organizational Values with Agile Principles

For an agile transformation to succeed at the cultural level, an organization's core values must align with the principles of agility. Agile isn't just a set of practices; it's a philosophy that prioritizes adaptability, collaboration, and continuous improvement. If these values aren't embedded in the organization's DNA, agile practices will struggle to take root, no matter how well individual teams adopt them.

Adaptability: At its core, agility is about responding quickly to change. Organizations that value adaptability are willing to pivot when necessary, recognizing that market conditions, customer needs, and business landscapes are constantly evolving. This requires a mindset shift, from rigid long-term planning to a more flexible approach where decisions are made iteratively, based on real-time data and feedback.

Trust and Collaboration: Agile thrives on collaboration, both within teams and across the organization. For this to happen, there must be a foundation of trust. When employees trust leadership and each other, they are more likely to engage in open communication, take risks, and offer creative solutions. Organizations that emphasize collaboration across departments, rather than fostering competition, enable agile teams to work more cohesively and drive better outcomes.

Customer-Centricity: Agile organizations are deeply focused on delivering value to the customer. This means shifting from an internal, process-oriented mindset to one that prioritizes customer needs and experiences. When an organization's values are aligned with customer-centricity, agile practices—like delivering incremental value and gathering continuous feedback—become natural extensions of the way the company operates.

By aligning organizational values with these agile principles, companies create an environment where agility can flourish. Leaders play a crucial role in reinforcing these values through their actions and decisions, ensuring that they aren't just words on a wall but lived realities in the workplace.

Breaking Down Silos and Encouraging Cross-Departmental Collaboration

One of the greatest challenges to fostering agility across an organization is the existence of silos. In traditional organizations, departments often operate independently, with little communication or collaboration between them. While this might have worked in the past, it stifles agility by slowing down decision-making, creating bottlenecks, and preventing teams from seeing the bigger picture.

To cultivate a truly agile culture, organizations must break down these silos and promote cross-departmental collaboration. Here are some key strategies for achieving this:

Create Cross-Functional Teams: One of the most effective ways to eliminate silos is to create cross-functional teams that bring together individuals from different departments. These teams can work on projects collaboratively, combining expertise from areas like marketing, development, sales, and customer support. Cross-functional teams ensure that different perspectives are represented and that solutions are more holistic and better aligned with customer needs.

Foster a Unified Vision: Collaboration across departments is easier when there's a shared sense of purpose. Leaders can promote this by communicating a clear, unified vision for the organization that everyone understands and supports. When employees from different areas of the company are working toward the same goals, it breaks down the barriers that often separate departments and encourages collective ownership of success.

Encourage Transparency and Communication: Silos often form because departments aren't communicating effectively. Leaders must encourage open dialogue between teams, providing platforms and tools that facilitate cross-departmental communication. Regular company-wide updates, shared dashboards, and collaborative meetings can help ensure that information flows freely across the organization.

By breaking down silos and encouraging collaboration between departments, organizations can create a more cohesive, agile culture. When everyone is aligned, working together, and focused on shared goals, the company becomes more responsive, innovative, and capable of delivering real value to its customers.

Embedding Continuous Improvement and Learning

A culture of agility thrives on continuous improvement and learning. Agile organizations are always seeking ways to evolve, adapt, and refine their processes, ensuring that they stay ahead in a rapidly changing business landscape. But fostering a culture of continuous improvement requires more than just implementing agile practices—it involves creating an environment where learning and growth are embedded into the daily work experience.

Promoting a Growth Mindset: Agile organizations encourage a growth mindset at every level, from leadership to frontline employees. A growth mindset is the belief that skills and abilities can be developed through effort and learning. This contrasts with a fixed mindset, where individuals believe their talents are innate and unchangeable. By promoting a growth mindset, organizations empower employees to take risks, learn from failures, and continuously seek out new ways to improve. In this type of environment, mistakes are not seen as setbacks, but as valuable opportunities for learning.

Regular Retrospectives: Agile teams conduct regular retrospectives, where they reflect on what worked well, what didn't, and how they can improve in the future. This practice is essential to creating a cycle of continuous improvement. However, retrospectives shouldn't be limited to individual teams—organizations as a whole can benefit from applying this principle across departments and leadership levels. By regularly reviewing processes, performance, and outcomes, companies can identify areas for improvement and make adjustments that enhance efficiency and collaboration.

Encouraging Experimentation: Agile organizations don't wait for perfect solutions—they experiment, iterate, and learn along the way. Encouraging experimentation allows teams to explore new ideas, test hypotheses, and innovate without fear of failure. Leaders should support this mindset by giving teams the freedom to try new approaches and learn from both successes and failures. When experimentation is part of the company's DNA, agility becomes a natural outcome.

Investing in Learning and Development: Continuous improvement is only possible when employees have the tools and knowledge they need to grow. Organizations must invest in the learning and development of their workforce, offering training programs, workshops, and opportunities for employees to expand their skills. Whether through formal education or peer-to-peer knowledge sharing, agile organizations prioritize learning as a core part of their culture.

By embedding continuous improvement and learning into the organizational fabric, companies ensure that they remain adaptable, innovative, and prepared for future challenges. This commitment to growth helps create a resilient organization where agility isn't just a practice—it's a mindset.

Closing Thoughts

Fostering a culture of agility requires more than just implementing new processes—it demands a shift in the way organizations think, operate, and learn. Leaders play a crucial role in driving this transformation by modeling agile behaviors, aligning organizational values with agile principles, and encouraging cross-departmental collaboration.

By embedding continuous improvement and learning into the company's culture, organizations can create an environment where agility is not just possible but sustainable. As we move forward, the focus will shift to how organizations can measure the success of their agile transformations and ensure that these changes endure in the long term.

Case Study: Salesforce

Overview:

Salesforce, a global leader in customer relationship management (CRM) software, recognized the need to stay adaptable and innovative in an ever-changing market. To achieve this, Salesforce implemented **Agile practices** across its organization, shifting focus from rigid processes to delivering **incremental value**. This flexible approach empowered teams to innovate, respond quickly to market demands, and align development efforts with business goals.

The transformation process included:

- **Incremental Value Delivery:** Salesforce adopted a model where teams delivered smaller, usable increments of work more frequently. This approach ensured continuous value for customers and allowed the company to respond to feedback swiftly.
- **Flexible Agile Frameworks:** Rather than adhering strictly to one Agile framework, Salesforce encouraged flexibility in adopting elements of **Scrum, Kanban, and Lean**. This flexibility allowed teams to choose practices that best fit their workflows and objectives.
- **Innovation Sprints:** Teams were encouraged to dedicate time to innovation, fostering a culture of creativity and experimentation. This practice helped generate new ideas and improvements outside of regular product development.
- **Cross-Functional Collaboration:** By promoting collaboration across departments—including product management, design, engineering, and marketing—Salesforce broke down silos and improved internal communication. This alignment ensured that business goals and customer needs were at the center of development efforts.
- **Continuous Feedback and Adaptation:** Regular retrospectives, sprint reviews, and feedback loops enabled teams to continuously reflect, adapt, and improve processes, ensuring they remained aligned with business objectives.

Challenges Faced:

Salesforce's transformation required a cultural shift away from traditional, process-heavy methodologies. Initial resistance to change and the need to balance flexibility with consistency posed challenges. Through strong leadership support, continuous coaching, and a commitment to Agile principles, these challenges were addressed over time.

Outcome:

The Agile transformation at Salesforce delivered impressive results:

- **Significant Business Growth:** By focusing on delivering incremental value and responding to customer feedback, Salesforce was able to accelerate product development, leading to sustained business growth and competitive advantage.
- **Enhanced Internal Collaboration:** Cross-functional teams worked more effectively, resulting in better alignment, faster decision-making, and improved problem-solving.
- **Increased Innovation:** The emphasis on flexible processes and innovation sprints fostered a culture where creativity thrived. Teams felt empowered to experiment, leading to innovative solutions and continuous product improvements.
- **Adaptability to Market Demands:** Salesforce's ability to pivot quickly in response to market needs ensured that the company remained agile and resilient, maintaining its leadership position in the CRM industry.

Salesforce's experience underscores how aligning Agile values with business goals can drive growth, foster innovation, and strengthen internal collaboration. The company's success highlights the power of trust, empathy, and empowerment in enabling a dynamic and adaptable organization.

Key Takeaway:

Salesforce's journey demonstrates that by embracing flexibility, incremental value delivery, and cross-functional collaboration, organizations can achieve significant growth and innovation. Trust, empathy, and empowerment are essential in sustaining an Agile culture and aligning development efforts with business success.

Why: The Apollo 11 mission team demonstrates agility and adaptability, as their success in landing a man on the moon required quick thinking, continuous improvement, and cross-team collaboration in an extremely high-stakes environment.

CHAPTER 6

Measuring Success and Sustaining Agile Transformation

"You can't improve what you don't measure."
— Peter Drucker

Introduction

An agile transformation isn't a one-time event—it's an ongoing journey that requires regular evaluation and adaptation. While implementing agile practices can lead to immediate improvements, sustaining these changes over the long term requires continuous effort. To ensure that agile transformation is delivering real value, organizations must measure their progress and success in meaningful ways.

Measuring success in agile goes beyond simply tracking project completion. It's about evaluating how well teams are collaborating, how quickly the organization can respond to changes, and how satisfied both customers and employees are with the outcomes. By focusing on the right metrics, organizations can gain valuable insights into the effectiveness of their agile initiatives and identify areas for improvement. Measurement is not just a way to track performance—it's a tool for continuous improvement and long-term sustainability.

Key Metrics for Agile Success

To assess the success of agile transformation, organizations need to track a combination of qualitative and quantitative metrics. These metrics should align with the organization's goals and provide actionable insights into how well agile practices are driving value. Below are some of the most important metrics to consider:

Lead Time and Cycle Time

- **Lead time** measures the total time it takes to complete a task, from the moment it's requested to the moment it's delivered. **Cycle time**, on the other hand, focuses on the time it takes to

complete the work once it's started. Both metrics are critical for understanding how efficiently teams are working.
- By reducing lead time and cycle time, teams can deliver value to customers faster. These metrics help identify bottlenecks in processes and provide insights into where improvements can be made to speed up delivery without sacrificing quality.

Team Velocity

- Team velocity measures the amount of work a team can complete in a given sprint or iteration. By tracking velocity over time, teams can gauge their capacity and predict how much work they can handle in future sprints.
- It's important to use velocity as a relative measure, not a hard target. Rather than focusing solely on increasing velocity, teams should aim for consistency and improvement. Fluctuations in velocity can provide insights into issues like over-committing, underestimating work, or inefficiencies in the workflow.

Customer Satisfaction

- Agile is ultimately about delivering value to the customer, so customer satisfaction is a key indicator of success. Regular feedback from customers—through surveys, interviews, or direct feedback loops—provides valuable insights into how well the product or service is meeting customer needs.
- Tools like Net Promoter Score (NPS) or customer satisfaction surveys can be used to gauge customer sentiment. By continuously measuring and responding to customer feedback, agile teams can make adjustments that improve the customer experience.

Employee Engagement

- Agile success isn't just about output; it's also about team health and morale. Engaged employees are more productive, collaborative, and innovative. Measuring employee engagement through surveys, one-on-one check-ins, or team retrospectives can help leaders understand how motivated and satisfied their teams are.
- High levels of engagement often correlate with better team performance, as engaged employees are more likely to take ownership of their work and contribute to continuous improvement efforts.

By tracking these key metrics, organizations can gain a clearer picture of how well their agile transformation is progressing. These measurements help teams make informed decisions, optimize processes, and ensure that agile practices are delivering meaningful results.

Creating Feedback Loops

In agile, feedback loops are essential for continuous learning and adaptation. They allow organizations to stay responsive to customer needs, team dynamics, and shifting business conditions. By embedding feedback loops into every stage of the process, organizations can ensure they remain agile, adaptable, and aligned with their goals.

Customer Feedback: Agile teams prioritize delivering value to customers, which makes customer feedback a crucial part of the agile process. Whether through regular check-ins, product demos, or user testing, feedback from customers helps teams understand how well their solutions are addressing real-world needs. Early and frequent customer feedback ensures that the team is always moving in the right direction, minimizing the risk of delivering a product that misses the mark.

Team Retrospectives: At the end of each sprint or iteration, agile teams hold retrospectives to reflect on their performance. These sessions provide a safe space for team members to discuss what went well, what didn't, and how they can improve moving forward. Retrospectives are one of the most important feedback loops in agile because they help teams identify bottlenecks, inefficiencies, or collaboration issues and then adjust accordingly.

Leadership Reviews: Leadership also plays a role in the feedback process. Regular leadership reviews, where executives and team leaders assess the progress of agile initiatives, help ensure that the organization's goals and strategies remain aligned. These reviews create opportunities for adjusting priorities, reallocating resources, or refining strategies based on the outcomes of agile projects. Transparent leadership reviews also signal that the organization is committed to agility at every level.

By building robust feedback loops into every part of the agile process, organizations can continually refine their work, improve team dynamics, and ensure they are delivering value to customers. Feedback isn't just something that happens at the end of a project—it's an ongoing process that informs each decision and action.

Sustaining Agile Transformation

While the initial excitement of an agile transformation can drive momentum, sustaining that transformation over the long term requires continued effort and focus. Without sustained commitment, organizations risk falling back into old habits or treating agile as a set of tools rather than a cultural shift. Below are strategies for maintaining agile momentum and ensuring lasting success.

Ongoing Leadership Support: Agile transformation begins with leadership, but it also needs ongoing support to thrive. Leaders must remain engaged, providing the vision, resources, and encouragement that teams need to continue improving. This means actively participating in retrospectives, celebrating wins, and remaining open to feedback. Leadership should consistently reinforce the value of agile practices, making it clear that agility is an organizational priority.

Investing in Team Development: Agile teams must continue to grow and develop if they are to sustain their effectiveness. This requires investment in training, coaching, and opportunities for professional growth. Agile organizations should provide teams with the resources they need to deepen their skills, experiment with new tools, and adopt emerging best practices. Investing in team development ensures that teams remain innovative, adaptable, and capable of tackling new challenges.

Celebrating Wins and Reinforcing Agile Values: Celebrating milestones and successes helps maintain morale and keeps teams motivated. Leaders should recognize and reward agile practices that contribute to the organization's goals, whether through faster delivery, higher customer satisfaction, or improved collaboration. Reinforcing agile values in everyday work strengthens the agile culture and keeps it alive in the long term.

Addressing Common Challenges: Sustaining an agile transformation also means addressing challenges as they arise. Organizations may face resistance to change, issues with scaling agile practices, or lapses in collaboration between teams. Leaders must remain vigilant, identifying and addressing these challenges early before they undermine the progress made during the initial transformation. By proactively managing these challenges, organizations can preserve the agility they've worked hard to cultivate.

Sustaining an agile transformation requires persistence, but the rewards—greater innovation, adaptability, and customer satisfaction—make the effort worthwhile. By continuing to invest in agile practices, organizations can build a resilient, forward-thinking culture that thrives in an ever-changing business landscape.

The Importance of Flexibility

One of the core principles of agile is flexibility. In a constantly evolving business environment, organizations must remain nimble, adapting their strategies, processes, and even their culture to meet changing demands. While adopting agile practices can help build this flexibility, organizations must also recognize that agile itself isn't static. What works today may not work tomorrow, and sustaining agility requires a willingness to continuously evolve.

Agile is Not One-Size-Fits-All: Organizations must recognize that agility looks different depending on the context. What works for one team or department may need to be adjusted for another. Flexibility means allowing teams to adapt agile frameworks like Scrum, Kanban, or Lean to suit their unique needs while staying aligned with the broader organizational goals. Leaders should encourage teams to experiment with different approaches and refine their practices as they learn what works best for them.

Revisiting Processes Regularly: As organizations grow and change, it's essential to periodically revisit and assess agile practices. Teams should ask themselves: Are our processes still effective? Are we truly delivering value to the customer? Regular reviews of agile practices ensure that teams remain focused on continuous improvement and don't become complacent. Agility requires the constant refinement of processes to maintain efficiency and effectiveness.

Staying Open to New Approaches: Flexibility also means being open to adopting new tools, technologies, or methodologies as they emerge. The agile landscape continues to evolve, with new practices and innovations being introduced regularly. By staying curious and open to change, organizations can ensure they are leveraging the latest advancements to stay competitive. Agile leaders should create a culture that welcomes innovation and encourages teams to explore new ways of working.

Ultimately, agility is about embracing change—not just in terms of project work but in how the organization itself operates. Flexibility ensures that organizations don't just become agile, but stay agile over the long term.

Closing Thoughts

Measuring success and sustaining an agile transformation requires continuous commitment to improvement, flexibility, and alignment with organizational goals. Agile isn't a destination—it's a journey that evolves as the business and market conditions change. By focusing on key metrics, building strong feedback loops, and maintaining flexibility, organizations can ensure that their agile transformation delivers lasting value.

As we conclude this exploration of agile transformation, it's clear that adopting an agile mindset is about more than just implementing new processes. It's about reshaping the way we lead, collaborate, and innovate. With the right approach, agility can become a core strength that empowers organizations to thrive in an ever-changing world.

Case Study: MeVis Medical Solutions

Overview:

MeVis Medical Solutions, a software company specializing in medical imaging solutions, faced challenges related to **technical debt, slow productivity**, and the need for higher-quality outputs. To address these issues, MeVis implemented **Scrum** as part of its Agile transformation. This initial adoption yielded positive results, prompting the company to bring in an **Agile consulting service** to further optimize processes and sustain improvements.

The transformation process involved:

- **Reducing Technical Debt:** By adopting Scrum practices such as sprint planning, daily stand-ups, and retrospectives, MeVis focused on identifying and addressing technical debt incrementally. Prioritizing technical debt alongside new development ensured more sustainable and maintainable codebases.
- **Continuous Improvement:** The use of retrospectives allowed teams to reflect on challenges and improve their workflows regularly. This feedback loop fostered a culture of continuous improvement and learning.
- **Agile Consulting Support:** To build on early successes, MeVis engaged Agile consultants who provided expert guidance, training, and coaching. This support helped refine their Agile practices and address deeper systemic issues.
- **Team Empowerment:** Scrum's focus on self-organizing teams gave employees more autonomy and ownership over their work. This empowerment improved morale and motivated teams to deliver higher-quality solutions.

- **Customer-Centric Focus:** The iterative delivery approach ensured that customer feedback was incorporated frequently, allowing MeVis to develop products that better met the needs of end users.

Challenges Faced:

The initial Scrum implementation required a shift in mindset and practices, which met some resistance. Additionally, balancing technical debt reduction with ongoing product development was challenging. The involvement of Agile consultants helped address these issues by providing tailored strategies and ongoing support.

Outcome:

MeVis Medical Solutions achieved significant improvements through their Agile transformation:

- **Increased Productivity:** Teams experienced a **10-15% increase** in productivity due to better workflow management, clearer priorities, and reduced technical debt.
- **Reduced Technical Debt:** By addressing technical debt consistently, MeVis improved code quality, system stability, and maintainability.
- **Enhanced Customer Satisfaction:** The focus on iterative delivery and customer feedback led to products that better met user needs, improving overall satisfaction.
- **Improved Internal Morale:** The shift to empowered, self-organizing teams created a more positive work environment, boosting employee morale and engagement.

MeVis's experience highlights the value of adopting Scrum and leveraging expert consulting to sustain Agile practices. The company's commitment to reducing technical debt, continuous improvement, and team empowerment led to tangible business results.

Key Takeaway:

MeVis Medical Solutions' journey demonstrates how implementing Scrum and seeking expert Agile support can lead to significant productivity gains, reduced technical debt, and improved customer satisfaction. Trust, empathy, and empowerment are key drivers in sustaining these improvements and fostering a culture of continuous growth.

Why: Henry Ford's development of the assembly line revolutionized manufacturing. It's an example of how measuring success (increased production efficiency) led to sustained improvement in industrial processes, much like agile's continuous improvement.

CHAPTER 7

Overcoming Challenges in Agile Transformation

"The greatest glory in living lies not in never falling, but in rising every time we fall."
— Nelson Mandela

Introduction

While agile transformation can bring significant benefits, it's not without its challenges. Organizations often encounter resistance, face difficulties scaling agile across teams, and struggle to maintain alignment between their agile practices and business goals. These obstacles can slow down progress or even threaten to derail the transformation entirely.

However, with the right strategies and mindset, these challenges can be overcome. Agile is about adaptability—not just in delivering projects, but in navigating the bumps along the transformation journey itself. This chapter will explore some of the most common challenges organizations face during their agile transformation and provide practical solutions for addressing them.

Resistance to Change

One of the most common challenges in any transformation, including agile, is resistance to change. Agile requires teams to work in new ways, and for some employees, this shift can feel threatening or uncomfortable. People naturally resist change, especially when it challenges long-standing habits or requires them to step out of their comfort zone.

Resistance often stems from a few key factors:

Fear of Losing Control: In traditional organizations, managers and leaders are used to having control over decisions and processes. Agile shifts much of that decision-making power to teams, which can make some leaders feel like they're losing control. Employees, too, may fear that agile will change their roles or make their contributions less visible.

Comfort with the Status Quo: For employees who have worked in traditional environments for a long time, agile may seem disruptive. People are often comfortable with familiar processes, even if they aren't the most efficient. Changing how they work can lead to uncertainty and stress, leading to pushback.

Lack of Understanding: Resistance can also come from a lack of understanding about what agile really is and how it works. Without proper education and communication, employees may see agile as just another management trend or feel that it's being forced on them without clear benefits.

Overcoming Resistance

Clear Communication: The first step in overcoming resistance is to communicate clearly and consistently about why the organization is adopting agile. Leaders must explain the benefits of agile—not just for the company, but for individual employees as well. Highlighting how agile can make work more collaborative, efficient, and fulfilling can help ease concerns and win buy-in.

Involve Employees Early: People are more likely to embrace change when they feel involved in the process. Leaders should invite employees to participate in the planning and implementation of agile practices. By seeking their input and addressing their concerns early on, leaders can reduce resistance and foster a sense of ownership over the transformation.

Provide Training and Support: Many employees resist agile simply because they don't understand it or feel unprepared for the shift. Providing comprehensive training on agile methodologies, tools, and roles can help demystify the process and give employees the confidence they need to succeed in an agile environment. Ongoing support, such as coaching and mentorship, is also crucial to helping employees adapt to new ways of working.

Celebrate Early Wins: Celebrating early successes can help alleviate resistance by showing tangible proof that agile works. When teams see the benefits—faster decision-making, improved collaboration, or better customer outcomes—they're more likely to buy into the process. Leaders should make a point to recognize and celebrate these wins to build momentum.

Scaling Agile Across the Organization

While many organizations successfully adopt agile within individual teams, scaling agile across an entire organization presents unique challenges. Larger companies, especially those with traditional structures and processes, often struggle to apply agile practices at scale. The transition from a few agile teams to a fully agile organization requires more than just replicating what works at the team level—it demands a deliberate, strategic approach to ensure that agility is embedded across departments and functions.

Several common challenges arise when scaling agile:

Fragmentation: As more teams adopt agile, there's a risk that they will become siloed, each working in isolation with their own interpretation of agile practices. This can lead to inconsistencies in processes, misaligned priorities, and a breakdown in communication between teams.

Traditional Structures: Many organizations are still structured around hierarchical, top-down decision-making, which can conflict with agile's emphasis on team autonomy. Departments such as finance, HR, and marketing may not be familiar with agile methodologies, creating friction when trying to align their processes with agile teams.

Lack of Coordination: Without proper coordination, agile teams may pursue different goals or priorities, leading to confusion and inefficiency at the organizational level.

Strategies for Scaling Agile

Adopt a Scaling Framework: One effective way to scale agile is by adopting a structured framework designed specifically for larger organizations. Frameworks like the **Scaled Agile Framework (SAFe)** or **Large-Scale Scrum (LeSS)** provide guidance on how to manage multiple agile teams working across different projects and functions. These frameworks introduce roles and processes to ensure alignment while preserving the autonomy of individual teams.

Promote Cross-Team Collaboration: Scaling agile requires breaking down silos and encouraging cross-team collaboration. Regular meetings that bring together representatives from different teams can help ensure alignment on goals and priorities. Cross-functional teams, which include members from different departments, can also facilitate collaboration and ensure that agile practices are implemented consistently across the organization.

Ensure Leadership Buy-In: Agile transformation at scale requires strong support from leadership. Executives must be committed to driving agile practices across the entire organization, not just within isolated teams. This includes removing barriers, providing resources, and continuously reinforcing the importance of agility as a company-wide priority.

Provide Consistent Training and Support: Scaling agile successfully means ensuring that everyone—whether they're in a technical role, a support function, or a leadership position—understands agile principles. Consistent training across teams and departments ensures that the entire organization is on the same page, reducing confusion and increasing the likelihood of a successful transformation.

Maintaining Alignment Between Teams

As organizations scale agile, one of the key challenges is ensuring that all teams remain aligned—not just with each other, but with the organization's overall goals and strategy. Agile teams operate with a high degree of autonomy, which can sometimes lead to misalignment if there's no structure in place to keep them focused on shared objectives.

The Importance of Alignment

Alignment is critical because, while individual teams may be working on different projects, they are all contributing to the broader goals of the organization. When teams are aligned, they can collaborate more effectively, avoid duplication of effort, and ensure that their work adds value at the organizational level. Without alignment, teams risk working in isolation, leading to inefficiencies and a lack of cohesion.

Strategies for Maintaining Alignment

Regular Communication Across Teams: Frequent communication between teams is essential for maintaining alignment. Leaders should establish regular cross-team meetings, where teams can share progress, discuss challenges, and align on key priorities. This fosters collaboration and ensures that all teams are working toward the same goals.

Shared Goals and Objectives: One of the most effective ways to maintain alignment is by setting shared goals and objectives that teams can work toward collectively. This ensures that, while each team may be pursuing different initiatives, they are all contributing to the same broader objectives. Using OKRs (Objectives and Key Results) or similar goal-setting frameworks can help teams stay aligned with the organization's strategic priorities.

Leadership Guidance: Leadership plays a critical role in maintaining alignment across agile teams. By providing clear direction and reinforcing the organization's goals, leaders help teams stay focused and ensure that their efforts are contributing to the larger vision. Leaders should also regularly check in with teams to ensure that alignment is being maintained.

Dealing with Setbacks and Failures

Setbacks and failures are inevitable in any transformation, and agile transformations are no exception. Whether it's a failed sprint, a misaligned project, or a team struggling to adapt to new processes, setbacks can disrupt progress and shake confidence in the agile approach. However, agile is built on the principle of continuous improvement, which means failures are not the end—they're opportunities to learn, adapt, and improve.

Understanding the Nature of Failures in Agile

Failures in agile often occur when teams are pushing boundaries, experimenting with new ideas, or adjusting to a new way of working. In this sense, failure is a natural part of innovation. Agile encourages teams to "fail fast" and "fail small"—that is, to identify mistakes quickly, learn from them, and course-correct before the failure escalates into something larger. This iterative approach helps teams avoid catastrophic failures and keep moving forward.

Strategies for Overcoming Setbacks

Conduct Blameless Retrospectives: After a setback, it's important to conduct a retrospective to analyze what went wrong, without assigning blame. The goal is to create a safe space where the team can discuss the failure openly and honestly, identifying the root cause and determining how to prevent similar issues in the future. By focusing on solutions rather than fault, teams can use failures as valuable learning opportunities.

Pivot and Adapt: One of the strengths of agile is its flexibility. When teams encounter a setback, they have the ability to pivot and try a different approach. This might mean adjusting the scope of a project, changing priorities, or revisiting the team's processes to find a better way forward. Agile's emphasis on adaptability allows teams to respond to setbacks quickly and with confidence.

Support from Leadership: When failures occur, leaders play a critical role in maintaining team morale and supporting the learning process. Instead of viewing setbacks as a sign of weakness, agile leaders should encourage teams to learn from mistakes, celebrate the insights gained, and provide the resources needed to move forward. Leaders who show support during challenging times foster a culture of resilience and continuous improvement.

Focus on Incremental Wins: In the face of setbacks, it's important to focus on small, incremental wins that build momentum and restore confidence. Celebrating even minor successes helps teams stay motivated and reinforces the agile principle of delivering value in small, frequent increments. These small victories can help shift the focus away from the setback and reignite a sense of progress.

Closing Thoughts

Overcoming challenges is an essential part of any agile transformation journey. From resistance to change to scaling agile practices across the organization, teams and leaders must remain flexible, persistent, and focused on continuous improvement. Setbacks are not roadblocks; they are opportunities to learn, adapt, and refine the agile process.

By maintaining alignment, fostering cross-team collaboration, and staying committed to the principles of agility, organizations can successfully navigate the obstacles they encounter and emerge stronger, more resilient, and better equipped to thrive in an ever-changing environment.

Case Study: Lake.com

Overview:

Lake.com, a vacation rental company, encountered significant challenges as it managed **rapid growth** and sought to scale its business operations. The need for efficient processes, innovative solutions, and improved customer service became increasingly apparent. To address these challenges, Lake.com adopted **Scrum** to enhance its ability to develop and deploy new solutions, such as implementing **keyless entry systems** for properties.

The transformation process involved:

- **Implementing Scrum Framework:** By adopting Scrum practices like sprint planning, daily stand-ups, sprint reviews, and retrospectives, Lake.com created a structured and iterative approach to handling tasks and projects. This helped teams stay aligned, focused, and adaptable.

- **Scaling for Growth:** As the company grew, Scrum facilitated the management of complex projects and new business demands. Teams were able to prioritize tasks effectively, ensuring that critical features and services were delivered on time.
- **Introducing Keyless Entry Systems:** One of the key solutions implemented during this transformation was the integration of keyless entry systems. Scrum's iterative development allowed for rapid testing, feedback, and deployment of this feature, enhancing the convenience and security of Lake.com's services.
- **Enhancing Team Collaboration:** Cross-functional teams, consisting of developers, customer service representatives, and operations staff, collaborated closely to address challenges and deliver solutions. This approach reduced silos and improved communication across departments.
- **Continuous Feedback and Adaptation:** Regular retrospectives enabled teams to continuously refine processes and respond to customer feedback, ensuring ongoing improvement and alignment with business goals.

Challenges Faced:

Managing rapid growth required a significant shift in how Lake.com handled projects and customer service. The transition to Scrum demanded changes in workflows, team structures, and communication patterns. Initial resistance to change and the need for ongoing training were addressed through leadership support and coaching.

Outcome:

Lake.com's adoption of Agile methods led to significant improvements:

- **Increased Flexibility:** Scrum enabled the company to adapt quickly to new challenges and opportunities, making it easier to scale operations effectively.
- **Enhanced Services:** The successful implementation of keyless entry systems improved the overall guest experience by offering greater convenience and security.
- **Improved Customer Satisfaction:** Faster delivery of new solutions and a focus on customer feedback resulted in higher satisfaction levels among guests and property owners.
- **Team Efficiency:** Cross-functional collaboration and iterative development improved productivity, alignment, and morale within the teams.

Lake.com's experience highlights how adopting Scrum can empower growing companies to manage complexity, innovate efficiently, and enhance customer service.

Key Takeaway:

Lake.com's journey demonstrates that Agile practices like Scrum can provide the flexibility, collaboration, and efficiency needed to scale a business during periods of rapid growth. Trust, empathy, and empowerment are essential in sustaining these improvements and delivering outstanding customer experiences.

Why: The fall of the Berlin Wall symbolizes overcoming a monumental challenge and represents transformation on a massive scale. This image serves as a metaphor for breaking down barriers to change within organizations.

CHAPTER 8

Agile Tools and Technologies

"Technology is best when it brings people together."
— Matt Mullenweg

Introduction

Agile is not just a set of principles—it's also a practice that relies on efficient collaboration, transparency, and adaptability. To support these values, agile teams often use a variety of tools and technologies designed to streamline workflows, enhance communication, and provide real-time insights into project progress. While tools should never replace agile practices, they are essential for scaling agile across teams and ensuring that everyone stays aligned.

Selecting the right tools for your organization can make a significant difference in how smoothly your teams adopt agile. From managing backlogs to facilitating daily standups, the right technologies can enable teams to focus more on delivering value and less on managing tasks. In this chapter, we'll explore some of the most popular agile tools, their key features, and how to choose the best tools for your organization.

Popular Agile Tools

There's no shortage of tools available to support agile teams. The best tool for your organization depends on your team's size, the complexity of your projects, and the workflows you want to optimize. Below are some of the most popular tools used by agile teams, along with their key features and strengths.

Jira

Overview: Jira is one of the most widely used tools for agile project management, particularly for teams following Scrum or Kanban methodologies. Developed by Atlassian, Jira allows teams to manage their backlogs, track progress, and plan sprints in a highly customizable way.

Key Features:

- Comprehensive sprint planning and backlog management.
- Integration with various development tools.
- Burndown charts and velocity tracking for measuring team progress.

Best for: Larger teams that need robust tracking and reporting capabilities, especially in software development.

Trello

Overview: Trello is a simple, visually oriented tool that uses kanban boards to help teams organize tasks. Its drag-and-drop interface makes it intuitive and easy to use, even for teams new to agile.

Key Features:

- Visual task management with customizable boards, lists, and cards.
- Easy-to-use kanban-style workflow management.
- Integration with tools like Slack, Google Drive, and Confluence.

Best for: Small to medium-sized teams looking for a straightforward way to manage tasks and visualize progress.

Asana

Overview: Asana is a versatile project management tool designed to help teams coordinate work and track tasks. It's well-suited for teams that need to organize complex projects but also want flexibility in how they manage tasks.

Key Features:

- Customizable project views, including list, board, and calendar formats.
- Task dependencies, subtasks, and timeline management.
- Collaboration features like comment threads and file sharing within tasks.

Best for: Teams that need flexibility in organizing tasks and projects, particularly those working on complex, multi-faceted initiatives.

Slack

Overview: Slack is a communication tool that facilitates real-time collaboration. While not specifically designed for agile, it's widely used by agile teams for day-to-day communication, quick problem-solving, and staying connected, especially in remote or distributed teams.

Key Features:

- Channels for organizing team discussions.
- Integration with other agile tools like Jira, Trello, and Confluence.
- Instant messaging and video call capabilities for real-time collaboration.

Best for: Teams needing streamlined communication, particularly those that are distributed or working remotely.

Confluence

Overview: Also developed by Atlassian, Confluence is a knowledge-sharing platform that complements tools like Jira. It allows teams to create, share, and organize documentation, meeting notes, and project plans.

Key Features:

- Centralized space for project documentation and knowledge sharing.
- Integration with Jira for linking tasks and sprints to relevant documentation.
- Customizable templates for meeting notes, project planning, and retrospectives.

Best for: Teams that need a robust system for knowledge management and documentation, especially when working across multiple agile teams.

Key Features of Agile Tools

Agile tools are designed to help teams manage workflows, track progress, and collaborate effectively. While each tool has its own unique strengths, there are certain key features that every agile tool should offer to ensure it supports core agile practices. Below are some of the most important features to look for when choosing an agile tool:

Backlog Management

- A well-organized backlog is essential for agile teams to prioritize work and stay focused on delivering value. Agile tools should allow teams to create, manage, and prioritize product or sprint backlogs efficiently. Features like drag-and-drop prioritization, backlog filtering, and integration with user stories help teams stay on top of tasks and ensure that the most important work gets done first.

Sprint Planning and Tracking

- Agile teams work in short, iterative cycles known as sprints. Tools that support sprint planning make it easier for teams to define the scope of each sprint, assign tasks, and monitor progress in real time. This feature should also include sprint backlog views, task assignment, and capacity planning to help teams ensure they're committing to a realistic workload.
- Tracking progress during a sprint is equally important. Most agile tools offer dashboards or progress trackers that allow teams to see how much work has been completed and what remains. These insights help teams stay on track and adjust their approach if necessary.

Burndown Charts and Velocity Tracking

- Burndown charts visualize the amount of work remaining in a sprint or project, providing a clear snapshot of progress. Agile tools should include built-in burndown charts to help teams monitor progress and identify potential bottlenecks.
- Velocity tracking is another critical feature, as it shows the average amount of work a team completes over time. By tracking velocity, teams can make more accurate predictions about future sprints and plan accordingly.

Collaboration and Communication Features

- Agile tools should facilitate collaboration by allowing team members to share updates, comment on tasks, and provide feedback in real time. Integration with communication tools like Slack or Microsoft Teams is particularly helpful for

- distributed or remote teams, ensuring that everyone stays connected.
- Built-in comment threads, file sharing, and notifications help team members stay informed and aligned, reducing the need for lengthy meetings.

Integration with Other Systems

- Agile tools should integrate with other software systems your organization uses, such as development environments, document management tools, and communication platforms. Integration allows teams to streamline their workflows and avoid switching between multiple tools. For example, integrating Jira with Confluence ensures that documentation is linked directly to tasks, making it easy to access relevant information.

Choosing the Right Tools for Your Organization

With so many agile tools available, choosing the right one for your organization can be a challenge. The best tool for your team depends on several factors, including team size, project complexity, and the specific workflows you need to support. Below are some key considerations to help you select the right tool:

Team Size and Structure

- The size and structure of your team should guide your choice of tool. For small, self-organizing teams, simpler tools like Trello or Asana may be sufficient. These tools offer flexibility without overwhelming users with too many features. On the other hand, larger teams or organizations that need to manage multiple projects simultaneously may benefit from more robust tools like Jira, which offer advanced tracking and reporting capabilities.

Project Complexity

- Consider the complexity of your projects when choosing a tool. For straightforward projects with a limited number of tasks, a simple kanban board may be all you need. However, if your projects involve multiple sprints, dependencies, and cross-team collaboration, you'll need a tool that offers more sophisticated features like sprint planning, task dependencies, and backlog management.

Ease of Use

- No matter how powerful an agile tool is, it must be easy to use. A complicated, clunky interface can slow teams down and reduce productivity. Look for tools that offer intuitive navigation, clear visualizations, and customizable workflows. Ease of use is particularly important for teams that are new to agile, as it helps with adoption and engagement.

Scalability

- If your organization plans to scale agile across multiple teams or departments, it's important to choose a tool that can grow with you. Tools like Jira and Asana are well-suited for scaling, as they offer features that support cross-team collaboration, reporting, and integration with other systems. Scalability ensures that as your agile practices mature, your tool continues to meet your needs.

Integration with Existing Systems

- Consider how well the tool integrates with your existing software stack. For example, if your team uses Slack for communication, look for tools that can integrate with Slack to facilitate seamless collaboration. Integration reduces manual work and ensures that all relevant information is easily accessible, no matter which platform your team is using.

By considering these factors, you can choose the tool that best supports your agile teams and enables them to work efficiently and effectively.

Maximizing the Use of Agile Tools

Once you've chosen the right tools for your organization, the next step is to ensure that you're maximizing their potential. Agile tools are powerful, but to truly benefit from them, teams need to use them strategically. Below are some tips for getting the most out of your agile tools:

Regular Training and Onboarding

- To ensure that everyone on the team knows how to use the tools effectively, it's important to invest in regular training. Teams should be well-versed in the key features of the tools, such as sprint planning, task tracking, and reporting. For new team members, providing thorough onboarding to the tools is crucial to maintaining efficiency.
- As tools evolve, offering refresher courses or workshops can help teams stay up to date with new features and capabilities.

Customization to Fit Your Workflow

- Most agile tools offer customization options that allow teams to tailor workflows, boards, and reports to their specific needs. Taking the time to configure the tool according to how your team works will increase efficiency and ensure that the tool aligns with your processes.
- For example, customizing a kanban board in Trello to match your team's unique workflow or adjusting task categories in Asana to fit the way your team organizes work can help streamline project management.

Use Data to Drive Continuous Improvement

- Many agile tools offer rich data and reporting capabilities. Teams should leverage this data to drive continuous improvement by analyzing sprint performance, velocity, and other key metrics. Regularly reviewing burndown charts and velocity reports can help teams identify areas where they're excelling and where they can improve.
- Using these insights, teams can make more informed decisions about workload capacity, sprint goals, and task prioritization, ultimately improving both efficiency and output.

Encourage Team Collaboration

- Agile tools are most effective when they foster collaboration. Encourage team members to use features like task comments, file sharing, and real-time updates to keep communication flowing. Integrating your agile tool with communication platforms like Slack or Microsoft Teams can further enhance

collaboration by ensuring that everyone is aligned and has easy access to key project updates.
- Regularly using tools like Jira or Trello during standups and sprint reviews helps ensure that all team members are engaged and on the same page regarding progress and blockers.

Continuously Refine Usage Based on Feedback

- Agile teams should regularly solicit feedback on how well the tools are supporting their workflows. Are there features that aren't being used effectively? Are there bottlenecks that could be improved with better tool usage? By continuously refining how the tools are used, teams can make small adjustments that lead to significant improvements in productivity and collaboration.

Closing Thoughts

Agile tools play a crucial role in enabling teams to work efficiently, stay aligned, and continuously improve. However, the true value of these tools lies in how they're used. By selecting the right tools for your organization, customizing them to fit your workflows, and leveraging the data they provide, teams can maximize the benefits of agility and drive greater success.

As we move forward, the next chapter will explore how to sustain momentum after an agile transformation and ensure that agility remains a core part of the organization's long-term strategy.

Case Study: Microsoft

Overview:

Microsoft's Visual Studio team faced challenges with **streamlining their development process**, coordinating across multiple teams, and responding quickly to user feedback. To address these challenges, the team adopted **Scrum** to create a more iterative and collaborative approach to software development. By focusing on real-time feedback, continuous improvements, and team alignment, Microsoft aimed to accelerate development cycles and enhance product quality.

The transformation process included:

- **Scrum Implementation:** Microsoft's Visual Studio team adopted Scrum ceremonies such as sprint planning, daily stand-ups, sprint reviews, and retrospectives. This structured approach provided teams with clear goals, regular checkpoints, and opportunities for continuous improvement.
- **Real-Time Feedback:** The team integrated real-time feedback loops, enabling them to respond quickly to user needs and product issues. This responsiveness ensured that development efforts remained closely aligned with customer expectations.
- **Agile Tools and Automation:** Microsoft leveraged Agile tools and automated processes to improve workflow efficiency and reduce manual tasks. Tools like Azure DevOps supported sprint planning, task tracking, and collaboration, enhancing overall productivity.
- **Cross-Team Alignment:** Scrum practices facilitated better communication and coordination between different teams working on Visual Studio. This alignment ensured that

development efforts were synchronized and that dependencies were managed effectively.
- **Continuous Improvement:** Regular retrospectives allowed teams to reflect on their processes, identify challenges, and implement incremental improvements, fostering a culture of continuous learning and adaptation.

Challenges Faced:

The shift to Scrum required changes in team dynamics, communication practices, and project management processes. Initially, some teams struggled with adapting to the new iterative approach and real-time feedback mechanisms. However, through consistent leadership support, training, and iterative adjustments, these challenges were gradually overcome.

Outcome:

Microsoft's adoption of Scrum within the Visual Studio team led to significant improvements:

- **Faster Development Cycles:** The iterative nature of Scrum enabled more frequent releases and quicker delivery of new features, keeping Visual Studio competitive and responsive to user needs.
- **More Frequent Releases:** By streamlining their development process, the team was able to deliver updates and new versions more regularly, providing continuous value to users.
- **Improved Team Collaboration:** Scrum practices and Agile tools fostered greater transparency, communication, and alignment among team members, improving overall collaboration and efficiency.

- **Higher Product Quality:** Continuous feedback and iterative development helped the team identify and resolve issues early, resulting in higher-quality software and greater user satisfaction.

Microsoft's experience with Scrum highlights the power of Agile practices in driving efficiency, collaboration, and responsiveness in software development.

Key Takeaway:

Microsoft's Visual Studio team demonstrated that adopting Scrum and real-time feedback mechanisms can accelerate development cycles, improve collaboration, and enhance product quality. Trust, empathy, and empowerment are critical elements in sustaining these Agile practices and achieving lasting success.

Why: Steve Jobs' introduction of the iPhone is a historic moment in technological advancement and showcases the power of tools and technologies to revolutionize industries. It aligns with how agile tools enable organizations to evolve and adapt.

CHAPTER 9

Sustaining Agile Momentum

"Success is not final, failure is not fatal: It is the courage to continue that counts."
— Winston Churchill

Introduction

Successfully transforming an organization into an agile one is a significant achievement, but the real challenge lies in maintaining that momentum over the long term. After the initial excitement of the agile transformation fades, organizations must ensure that agility remains a core part of how they operate. Agility is not a one-time change; it's an ongoing journey that requires continuous effort, commitment, and refinement.

Sustaining agile momentum means embedding the principles of agility—like collaboration, adaptability, and continuous improvement—into the organization's culture. When these values become part of the company's DNA, agile practices will thrive and evolve naturally. In this chapter, we'll explore the strategies that help organizations maintain their agility and ensure that it delivers lasting value.

Embedding Agile Values into the Culture

For agile to truly take root, its values must extend beyond individual teams and become ingrained in the organization's culture. This cultural shift requires a deliberate effort to reinforce and model agile principles at every level of the organization. When agile values like transparency, collaboration, and adaptability are woven into the fabric of the company, they guide decision-making, drive behaviors, and ensure that agile practices are sustainable over time.

Leadership Reinforces the Values

Leaders play a critical role in embedding agile values into the culture. It's not enough to simply introduce agile practices—leaders must continuously reinforce these principles through their actions and communication. Leaders should model transparency by openly sharing goals, progress, and challenges with their teams. They should encourage collaboration by fostering an environment where cross-functional teams work together toward common goals, and adaptability by showing a willingness to pivot when conditions change.

By consistently reinforcing these values, leaders set the tone for the rest of the organization. When employees see agile principles in action at the highest levels, they're more likely to embrace and practice them in their own work.

Recognizing and Rewarding Agile Behaviors

To ensure that agile values are sustained, organizations must recognize and reward behaviors that align with these principles. Teams that demonstrate strong collaboration, adaptability, or continuous improvement should be celebrated, whether through public recognition, performance reviews, or other incentives. When employees see that agile behaviors are valued, they're more likely to continue practicing them.

This also applies to how organizations handle failure. In an agile culture, failure is viewed as a learning opportunity, not a setback. Leaders should celebrate teams that experiment, take risks, and learn from their mistakes, reinforcing the value of innovation and continuous improvement.

Embedding Agile into HR Processes

To make agile a lasting part of the culture, organizations should embed agile principles into HR processes such as hiring, onboarding, and performance evaluations. For example, hiring criteria should prioritize candidates who demonstrate flexibility, a collaborative mindset, and a willingness to adapt to change. Onboarding programs should introduce new employees to the company's agile values from day one, helping them understand how these principles guide the organization's operations.

Similarly, performance evaluations should assess how well employees embody agile values in their day-to-day work. By aligning HR processes with agile principles, organizations ensure that their culture evolves to support and sustain agility.

Continuous Improvement and Innovation

Agility is not just about adapting to change—it's about continuously seeking ways to improve and innovate. For organizations to sustain agile momentum, they must remain focused on fostering a culture of continuous improvement. Agile teams are designed to reflect, adapt, and evolve with each iteration, but for this to become part of the organization's DNA, leaders must actively promote the mindset of "always getting better."

Retrospectives as a Driver of Improvement

Regular retrospectives are one of the most powerful tools for continuous improvement. They provide teams with an opportunity to reflect on what went well, what didn't, and how they can improve moving forward. Retrospectives help teams identify inefficiencies, streamline workflows, and ensure that they are learning from each sprint or project. Organizations that make retrospectives a regular, meaningful part of their processes are more likely to embed continuous improvement into their culture.

To sustain momentum, teams must take actionable insights from their retrospectives and apply them consistently. Whether it's adjusting workflows, refining communication practices, or experimenting with new ideas, each improvement should lead to measurable changes that drive progress.

Encouraging Experimentation

Innovation thrives in environments where experimentation is encouraged. Agile organizations should create space for teams to try new ideas, test different approaches, and take calculated risks. Leaders can support this by fostering a "fail fast, learn fast" culture, where teams are encouraged to experiment without fear of punishment for mistakes.

By regularly creating opportunities for teams to experiment—whether through innovation sprints, hackathons, or dedicated time for creative problem-solving—organizations can keep agility alive and ensure that they are constantly pushing the boundaries of what's possible.

Learning from Failures

Failures are inevitable, but how an organization responds to failure can determine its long-term success. In agile organizations, failure is treated as a valuable learning opportunity. When teams analyze their failures through retrospectives or feedback sessions, they gain insights into what went wrong and how to avoid similar pitfalls in the future.

To sustain agile momentum, organizations must cultivate a mindset that sees failure as part of the process of improvement. Leaders should encourage open discussions about failures, celebrate the lessons learned, and ensure that teams are empowered to apply those lessons to future work.

Keeping Teams Engaged and Motivated

Maintaining team engagement and motivation is key to sustaining agile practices over the long term. Agile teams thrive on collaboration, autonomy, and the ability to make a meaningful impact. To keep teams engaged, organizations must prioritize a work environment where team members feel valued, supported, and challenged.

Recognizing Achievements and Celebrating Milestones

Recognition plays a critical role in maintaining motivation. Teams that are recognized for their hard work and achievements are more likely to stay engaged and committed to continuous improvement. Leaders should make it a point to regularly celebrate both small wins and major milestones, acknowledging the collective efforts of the team.

Whether it's hitting a project deadline, completing a successful sprint, or solving a complex problem, these moments of recognition help reinforce the importance of agile practices and keep team morale high.

Providing Opportunities for Growth

Agile teams are most effective when they are continuously learning and developing their skills. Providing team members with opportunities for personal and professional growth—whether through training programs, certifications, or hands-on learning—keeps them motivated and engaged. Leaders should work with team members to identify areas where they want to grow and offer resources that support their development.

Additionally, rotating roles within teams or providing stretch assignments can help employees build new skills and perspectives, keeping them engaged in their work and ensuring that the team remains flexible and adaptive.

Practicing Servant Leadership

Servant leadership plays an important role in keeping teams motivated over the long term. Servant leaders prioritize the needs of the team, removing roadblocks and providing the resources and support necessary for success. By fostering a culture of trust, empathy, and empowerment, servant leaders help create an environment where teams feel valued and motivated to give their best.

Regular one-on-one meetings, team check-ins, and feedback loops ensure that leaders stay connected with their teams, addressing concerns early and reinforcing the sense of shared ownership that is central to agile success.

Ensuring Leadership Commitment

Sustaining agile momentum requires continuous support and commitment from leadership. Leaders play a vital role in driving agility, not just by initiating the transformation but by staying actively engaged in its long-term success. Agile is not something that can be handed off to teams and forgotten—leaders must be visible champions of agile values and practices throughout the organization.

Continuous Reinforcement of Agile Principles

Leaders must consistently reinforce the importance of agile principles like adaptability, collaboration, and transparency. This reinforcement goes beyond verbal encouragement; it must be evident in the way leaders make decisions, communicate, and interact with teams. By embodying these values, leaders set the tone for the rest of the organization, showing that agility is not just a temporary initiative but a core part of how the business operates.

Active Participation in Agile Processes

Leadership engagement in agile processes is critical to maintaining momentum. Leaders should participate in sprint reviews, retrospectives, and planning sessions—not as directors, but as collaborators. By being involved, leaders gain firsthand insights into the challenges and successes of agile teams, allowing them to offer more relevant support and remove roadblocks. This active participation also signals to teams that their work is valued and that leadership is committed to their success.

Providing Resources and Removing Obstacles

For agile to thrive, teams need access to the right resources, whether it's tools, training, or additional personnel. Leaders are responsible for ensuring that teams have what they need to deliver value and continuously improve. Equally important, leaders must actively remove obstacles that slow down progress, such as bureaucratic processes, unclear priorities, or resource constraints.

By consistently prioritizing agility, leaders can prevent agile from being undermined by the very structures and processes it seeks to change. Leadership's role in removing barriers is essential to sustaining long-term agility.

Staying Open to Feedback

Just as agile teams thrive on feedback loops, so must leadership. Leaders should regularly seek feedback from teams on how well agile practices are working and what improvements can be made at the organizational level. This openness to feedback ensures that agile practices evolve alongside the organization's needs and that leadership remains aligned with the challenges and opportunities that teams face.

By staying connected to the pulse of the organization, leaders can make informed decisions that keep agile transformation on track.

Closing Thoughts

Sustaining agile momentum requires more than just a successful initial transformation—it demands ongoing commitment, continuous improvement, and a culture that supports agility at every level. Leaders must stay engaged, reinforce agile values, and ensure that teams remain motivated and supported. By embedding agility into the fabric of the organization, companies can not only maintain the progress they've made but continue to thrive in an ever-changing business landscape.

As we move forward, the final chapter will explore how to future-proof agile practices, ensuring that the organization stays adaptive and resilient in the face of new challenges.

Case Study: Ling App

Overview:

Ling, a language learning app, faced the challenge of rapidly evolving user needs and the demand for continuous innovation in the competitive ed-tech market. To meet these challenges, Ling adopted **Agile methodologies** to create a more responsive and iterative approach to product development. By focusing on **short sprints** and continuous feedback, the company aimed to enhance features like **voice recognition**, improve user experience, and accelerate product innovation.

The transformation process included:

- **Short Iterative Sprints:** Ling adopted short, focused sprints that allowed the development team to deliver incremental improvements frequently. This approach ensured that new features and updates could be tested and refined quickly.
- **Continuous Customer Feedback:** The company established regular feedback loops with users to understand their needs and pain points. This direct feedback was integrated into each sprint cycle, ensuring the product evolved in alignment with user expectations.
- **Feature Enhancements:** By using Agile, Ling improved core features like **voice recognition technology**, making the app more intuitive and effective for language learners. Each sprint provided an opportunity to test, refine, and enhance these features based on real user data.
- **Cross-Functional Collaboration:** Development, design, and marketing teams worked closely together, ensuring that all

aspects of the product—from functionality to user experience—were aligned and optimized.
- **Adaptability to Market Demands:** Agile allowed Ling to pivot quickly in response to market trends and competitor innovations, keeping the app relevant and competitive.

Challenges Faced:

Initially, the transition to Agile required a shift in mindset and workflow. Teams had to adapt to a faster-paced development cycle and learn to integrate continuous feedback effectively. Through coaching, training, and leadership support, these challenges were successfully managed, and the teams embraced the Agile process.

Outcome:

Ling's adoption of Agile methodologies led to remarkable results:

- **Accelerated Product Roadmap:** The use of short sprints allowed Ling to roll out new features and improvements faster, keeping the product roadmap dynamic and aligned with user needs.
- **Improved User Experience:** Continuous feedback and iterative development enhanced the overall user experience, making the app more engaging and effective for language learners.
- **Significant Company Growth:** Agile practices helped Ling stay competitive, attract more users, and drive substantial business growth.
- **Innovation and Responsiveness:** The ability to respond quickly to user feedback and market demands fostered a culture of innovation and adaptability within the company.

Ling's experience demonstrates the power of Agile in driving rapid development, improving user satisfaction, and supporting business growth.

Key Takeaway:

Ling's journey shows that Agile methodologies, with a focus on short sprints and continuous feedback, can accelerate product development, enhance user experience, and fuel company growth. Trust, empathy, and empowerment are vital in creating a responsive and innovative development culture.

Why: The fall of the Roman Empire serves as a cautionary tale about the dangers of losing momentum and becoming complacent. This image could symbolize what happens when an organization fails to sustain agility and adaptability.

CHAPTER 10

Future-Proofing Agile Practices

"It is not the strongest of the species that survive, nor the most intelligent, but the one most responsive to change."
— Charles Darwin

Introduction

As organizations evolve, so too must their agile practices. Agile is not a static methodology—it thrives on flexibility, adaptation, and continuous learning. To remain competitive in an ever-changing business environment, organizations must future-proof their agile practices, ensuring they can scale and adapt to new challenges, technologies, and market demands. Future-proofing agile means going beyond the initial transformation and building a framework that can withstand the test of time, ensuring agility remains a core strength.

In this chapter, we'll explore strategies for keeping agile practices resilient, including staying flexible, embracing emerging technologies, fostering a culture of learning, and scaling agile to meet future demands.

Staying Flexible and Adaptive

At the heart of agile is the principle of flexibility. Agile practices are designed to help teams respond quickly to change—whether that's a shift in customer expectations, new market trends, or technological advancements. To future-proof agile, organizations must stay committed to flexibility, ensuring that processes, tools, and workflows remain adaptable as the business landscape evolves.

Continual Process Evaluation

One of the key ways to maintain flexibility is through regular evaluation of agile processes. Agile teams should regularly review their workflows, asking questions like:

- Are our current processes still effective in achieving our goals?

- Are we responding quickly enough to new information or changes in the market?
- What adjustments can we make to improve efficiency or collaboration?

Leaders must encourage teams to revisit their workflows periodically, allowing them to fine-tune practices based on current conditions. For example, a process that worked well for a small team may need to be restructured as the organization grows. Agile is about evolving practices, and by staying open to continuous improvement, organizations can ensure that their agility doesn't become rigid or outdated.

Responding to Market and Customer Changes

Agile's greatest strength is its ability to respond to real-time feedback and change. Organizations must keep this core principle alive by actively monitoring shifts in customer needs, market trends, and competitive pressures. Flexibility means not just reacting to change but anticipating it, ensuring that teams are always one step ahead. Regularly engaging with customers and staying attuned to the broader market landscape allows agile teams to pivot quickly and deliver solutions that are always aligned with the current environment.

For leaders, this means creating an environment where change is expected and embraced. By promoting adaptability as a cultural value, organizations can ensure that their teams are ready to respond to challenges and opportunities with agility.

Leadership's Role in Flexibility

Leadership plays a critical role in maintaining flexibility. Agile leaders should model adaptability by staying open to new approaches, encouraging experimentation, and supporting teams in making necessary adjustments. Leaders must also be willing to pivot their strategies when market conditions or organizational goals shift, ensuring that agility is preserved at both the team and organizational levels.

Flexibility in leadership also means empowering teams to make decisions quickly, without unnecessary approval layers. By giving teams the autonomy to adapt their workflows and approaches as needed, leaders foster a culture where agility is truly embedded in the organization's DNA.

Embracing Emerging Technologies

As technology evolves at an unprecedented pace, organizations must embrace emerging technologies to enhance their agile practices and remain competitive. From artificial intelligence (AI) and machine learning to automation and cloud computing, these technologies offer new ways to improve efficiency, drive innovation, and deliver value faster.

Leveraging AI and Machine Learning for Better Decision-Making

AI and machine learning are transforming how businesses operate, and they can significantly enhance agile workflows. These technologies can analyze vast amounts of data, providing insights that help teams make better decisions. For example, AI-powered tools can predict project risks, recommend resource allocation, or even automate parts of the software testing process. By integrating AI into their agile workflows, teams can reduce manual work, identify patterns in customer behavior, and make data-driven decisions that improve project outcomes.

Automation for Streamlining Processes

Automation is another powerful tool that can support agile teams by eliminating repetitive, time-consuming tasks. Whether it's automating software testing, deployment processes, or task management, automation frees up teams to focus on higher-value work. Automated workflows can also reduce human error and ensure that processes are consistent and efficient.

For agile teams, automation enhances speed and flexibility, allowing them to deliver updates or releases more frequently. By automating routine tasks, teams can reduce bottlenecks and improve their ability to respond to changes quickly.

Cloud-Based Collaboration Tools

Cloud technology has revolutionized the way teams collaborate, particularly in distributed or remote work environments. Tools like Jira, Trello, and Asana are already integral to agile workflows, but cloud computing takes collaboration to the next level. Teams can access project data, update tasks, and collaborate in real-time, regardless of their location. The scalability of cloud-based tools ensures that agile practices can grow with the organization, supporting cross-functional teams as they expand.

By embracing these emerging technologies, agile organizations can enhance their ability to innovate, streamline workflows, and deliver value at a faster pace.

Fostering a Learning Culture

Agility isn't just about processes and tools—it's about cultivating a mindset of continuous learning and improvement. To future-proof agile practices, organizations must foster a culture where learning is encouraged, experimentation is supported, and teams are empowered to adapt and grow.

Promoting Lifelong Learning

In an agile environment, learning should never stop. Teams should be encouraged to pursue new skills, explore emerging trends, and continuously develop their expertise. This can be done through formal training programs, workshops, and access to resources like online courses or certifications. Agile organizations that invest in their people's growth are better equipped to stay ahead of industry trends and respond to changing demands.

Leaders should model this commitment to learning by staying informed about the latest developments in agile methodologies, technology, and industry trends. By making learning a core organizational value, leaders create an environment where teams are constantly evolving and improving.

Encouraging Experimentation and Innovation

A key part of fostering a learning culture is creating a space for experimentation. Agile teams thrive when they are given the freedom to test new ideas, try different approaches, and learn from failures. Leaders can support this by encouraging teams to take risks and experiment without fear of punishment. Whether it's dedicating time for innovation sprints, holding brainstorming sessions, or setting aside resources for creative problem-solving, encouraging experimentation keeps agile teams engaged and helps drive continuous improvement.

Knowledge Sharing and Collaboration

Agile organizations must also prioritize knowledge sharing to ensure that learning is collective, not just individual. Tools like Confluence or

Microsoft Teams can be used to create shared knowledge repositories, where teams document their learnings, best practices, and insights. Regularly scheduled knowledge-sharing sessions, such as lunch-and-learns or cross-team retrospectives, can help ensure that valuable lessons are spread across the organization.

By fostering a culture of learning, organizations empower their teams to stay curious, innovative, and adaptable—qualities that are essential for long-term agility.

Scaling Agile for the Future

As organizations grow and evolve, scaling agile practices becomes essential to ensure that agility isn't confined to isolated teams but is embedded across the entire organization. However, scaling agile introduces new challenges—maintaining alignment, ensuring consistency, and fostering collaboration across larger, more complex structures. To future-proof agile, organizations must have a strategic approach to scaling, ensuring that they maintain agility even as they grow.

Establishing Frameworks for Scaling Agile

Frameworks like the **Scaled Agile Framework (SAFe)** or **Large-Scale Scrum (LeSS)** provide structured approaches to scaling agile across multiple teams or departments. These frameworks introduce additional layers of coordination, ensuring that agile practices are consistent, yet adaptable, across larger organizations. They also provide mechanisms for managing dependencies between teams, ensuring that everyone stays aligned with broader business goals.

By adopting a scaling framework, organizations can maintain the flexibility and speed of agile while creating the structure needed to manage complexity at scale. These frameworks also help standardize practices across teams, making it easier to measure performance and ensure that teams are working toward common objectives.

Cross-Team Collaboration and Alignment

As agile practices scale, ensuring alignment between teams is critical. Agile thrives on collaboration, and as organizations grow, it becomes more challenging to maintain seamless communication and coordination. Regular cross-team meetings, alignment sessions, and shared goal-setting processes can help ensure that teams remain aligned with overall business objectives and with each other.

Leadership plays a key role in facilitating this alignment by providing clear, transparent communication about strategic goals and ensuring that teams have the tools and resources they need to collaborate effectively.

Retaining Agility Across Geographies

For organizations that operate across multiple geographies, maintaining agile practices can be particularly challenging. Distributed teams may face difficulties in communication, time zone differences, and cultural variations that affect collaboration. However, technology can bridge these gaps, and with the right tools, distributed teams can stay connected and aligned.

Cloud-based collaboration platforms, virtual meeting tools, and real-time project management systems can help distributed teams maintain the agility and flexibility that local teams enjoy. Leaders must ensure that even as the organization grows and spans new locations, agility remains a core part of its DNA.

By strategically scaling agile practices and ensuring collaboration and alignment, organizations can preserve the benefits of agility while growing and evolving.

Closing Thoughts

Future-proofing agile practices is an ongoing journey, one that requires organizations to stay flexible, embrace new technologies, and foster a culture of continuous learning. By scaling agile thoughtfully, maintaining alignment across teams, and promoting experimentation and innovation, organizations can ensure that agility remains a core strength, enabling them to thrive in an ever-changing business landscape.

As the world evolves, so too must agile practices. With the right mindset and strategies, organizations can not only sustain their agility but enhance it, positioning themselves for long-term success in the future.

Case Study: Spotify

Overview:

Spotify, the global music streaming platform, faced the challenge of maintaining agility while rapidly scaling its operations and adapting to an ever-changing market. As the company grew, traditional development models became inefficient, and maintaining alignment across multiple teams became increasingly complex. To future-proof their agile practices, Spotify developed a unique approach known as the **Spotify Model**, emphasizing flexibility, autonomy, and continuous learning.

The transformation process involved:

- **Tribes, Squads, Chapters, and Guilds:** Spotify restructured its teams into **Squads** (small, cross-functional teams), grouped into **Tribes** (collections of squads working on related areas). **Chapters** provided functional expertise within tribes, while **Guilds** allowed for cross-tribe knowledge sharing. This model enabled scalability without sacrificing agility.
- **Continuous Adaptation:** Spotify emphasized that their model was not static. Teams were encouraged to experiment, iterate, and adapt their practices to fit their evolving needs. This flexibility ensured that their agile processes remained relevant and effective.
- **Autonomy and Alignment:** Squads were given a high degree of autonomy to decide how to achieve their goals. However, they operated within a framework of shared company objectives, ensuring alignment without micromanagement. Leadership focused on providing context and removing obstacles rather than dictating solutions.
- **Embracing Emerging Technologies:** Spotify leveraged cloud infrastructure, automation, and data analytics to streamline operations and enhance decision-making. These technologies enabled faster development cycles, better resource allocation, and real-time feedback.
- **Fostering a Learning Culture:** Continuous learning was embedded in Spotify's culture. Regular retrospectives, hackathons, and innovation sprints encouraged experimentation and skill development. Knowledge-sharing practices ensured that learning was distributed across the organization.

Challenges Faced:

As Spotify scaled, maintaining cohesion and communication across numerous squads and tribes was challenging. Balancing autonomy with alignment required constant attention and adaptation. Additionally, keeping agile practices flexible while ensuring consistency was an ongoing effort. Leadership played a key role in addressing these challenges by promoting transparency, trust, and a willingness to evolve.

Outcome:

Spotify's approach to future-proofing agile practices resulted in several significant benefits:

- **Scalable Agility:** The Spotify Model allowed the company to scale while preserving the speed, flexibility, and innovation of smaller teams.
- **Faster Innovation Cycles:** Continuous experimentation and adaptation led to faster delivery of new features, keeping Spotify ahead of competitors.
- **Enhanced Collaboration:** The combination of autonomy and alignment fostered effective collaboration across squads, tribes, and the entire organization.
- **Resilience to Change:** By building flexibility and continuous learning into their agile practices, Spotify was able to respond quickly to market changes, new technologies, and customer feedback.

Spotify's experience highlights the importance of designing agile practices that can evolve with the organization. Their commitment to flexibility, emerging technologies, and a learning culture ensured that agility remained a core strength, even as the company scaled.

Key Takeaway:

Spotify's journey demonstrates that future-proofing agile practices requires a balance of autonomy, alignment, and continuous adaptation. By embracing change, leveraging technology, and fostering a culture of learning, organizations can sustain and enhance their agility over time.

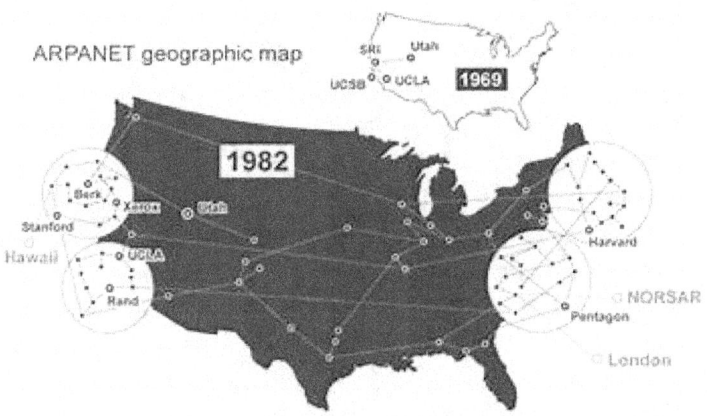

Why: The creation of ARPANET, which eventually evolved into the internet, is an example of a future-proof innovation that changed the world. It serves as an analogy for how agile organizations must anticipate and adapt to future challenges.

CHAPTER 11

Trust as the Foundation of Leadership

"Trust is the glue of life. It's the most essential ingredient in effective communication. It's the foundational principle that holds all relationships."
— Stephen Covey

Introduction

Trust is the foundation of effective leadership, and nowhere is this more evident than in servant leadership and agile environments. Without trust, collaboration falters, communication breaks down, and teams become disengaged. Trust enables leaders to create environments where employees feel safe to take risks, share ideas, and make decisions—core tenets of both agile practices and servant leadership.

In this chapter, we will explore why trust is not just a desirable quality in leadership but a critical necessity. We will delve into peer-reviewed research that highlights the role of trust in enhancing team cohesion, performance, and organizational success. Additionally, we'll examine practical ways leaders can build and maintain trust within their teams, creating the foundation for empowerment, innovation, and growth.

Why Trust is Critical in Leadership

Trust is often considered the glue that holds teams and organizations together. In leadership, trust is the bridge between vision and execution, providing the confidence teams need to perform at their best. When leaders establish trust, they unlock higher levels of collaboration, communication, and engagement.

Trust and Team Cohesion

Research consistently shows that trust plays a pivotal role in fostering team cohesion and improving performance. A study published in the *Journal of Organizational Behavior* found that teams with higher levels of trust were better able to collaborate, solve problems, and achieve goals. Trust enables team members to rely on each other's expertise and contributions, knowing that everyone is working toward a common goal. In the absence of trust, teams often become fragmented, with individuals prioritizing personal agendas over collective success.

In agile environments, where teams must work closely together to respond to change and deliver value incrementally, trust is even more critical. Agile teams need to collaborate in real-time, make decisions quickly, and share responsibility for outcomes. Trust allows them to do this confidently, without fear of blame or failure.

Psychological Safety and Innovation

Trust also creates the conditions for psychological safety, a concept popularized by researcher Amy Edmondson. Psychological safety refers to an environment where individuals feel safe to speak up, take risks, and express ideas without fear of ridicule or punishment. When teams feel psychologically safe, they are more likely to innovate and experiment, knowing that failure is part of the learning process.

In leadership, creating psychological safety begins with trust. Leaders who demonstrate trust in their teams—by allowing them to take ownership of decisions, offering support during failures, and fostering open communication—cultivate an environment where creativity and innovation can thrive. A study in the *Harvard Business Review* found that organizations with high psychological safety outperformed their peers in innovation and adaptability, particularly in fast-changing industries.

Trust and Employee Engagement

Trust is also directly linked to employee engagement and retention. According to a study published in the *International Journal of Business and Management*, employees who trust their leaders are more engaged, satisfied, and committed to their organizations. Trust in leadership has been shown to increase discretionary effort, as employees feel a greater sense of ownership and pride in their work.

Engaged employees are not only more productive but also more likely to stay with the organization long-term, reducing turnover and preserving institutional knowledge. In contrast, when trust is lacking, employees are more likely to disengage, leading to higher rates of absenteeism, reduced productivity, and increased turnover.

Building Trust as a Leader

Trust is not a given—it must be earned and continually nurtured. Leaders who prioritize trust-building can create an environment where their teams feel supported, valued, and empowered to take initiative. The following strategies can help leaders build and maintain trust within their teams:

Demonstrating Transparency and Vulnerability

Transparency is one of the most effective ways to build trust. Leaders who are open and honest about their decisions, challenges, and even their mistakes foster a sense of mutual respect within their teams. When leaders communicate openly about organizational goals, setbacks, and personal limitations, they humanize themselves and show that they trust their teams with the truth. This creates a culture of openness, where team members feel more comfortable sharing their own challenges and ideas.

Research published in the *Academy of Management Journal* shows that leaders who demonstrate vulnerability, such as admitting when they don't have all the answers, are more likely to build trust and stronger relationships with their teams. Vulnerability is not a sign of weakness—it's a pathway to deeper connections and trust.

Consistency and Integrity

Trust is built on consistency and integrity. Leaders who act in alignment with their stated values and consistently follow through on their promises demonstrate that they are reliable. This consistency creates a foundation of trust, as teams know that their leader's words and actions are congruent.

A study published in *Leadership Quarterly* found that integrity in leadership—defined as acting with honesty and moral principles—significantly enhances team trust. When employees perceive their leaders as acting fairly and with integrity, they are more likely to feel committed to the team's goals and objectives.

Empowering Teams and Delegating Responsibility

Trusting teams with decision-making authority is a powerful way to build trust. Leaders who micromanage or withhold responsibility signal a lack of trust, which can stifle creativity and demotivate teams. In contrast, leaders who delegate tasks and empower their teams to make decisions demonstrate that they trust their employees' judgment.

Empowerment fosters mutual trust. By trusting their teams to take ownership of their work, leaders build reciprocal trust, where employees feel more confident in their abilities and are motivated to perform at higher levels.

Providing Support and Accountability

Building trust doesn't mean abandoning accountability. Leaders must strike a balance between empowering teams and holding them accountable for results. Supportive leaders provide the resources, guidance, and feedback necessary for teams to succeed, while also setting clear expectations and holding them accountable for delivering on their commitments.

A supportive, accountable environment strengthens trust by ensuring that everyone is working toward the same goals, with clarity on roles and responsibilities. Teams trust leaders who have their back but also expect them to deliver results.

The Impact of Trust on Organizational Agility

Trust is the cornerstone of organizational agility. In agile environments, where teams must collaborate quickly and make decisions in real-time, trust enables speed and flexibility. Agile teams that operate in high-trust environments are more capable of adapting to change, experimenting with new ideas, and delivering results faster.

Faster Decision-Making

Trust enables agile teams to make decisions quickly, without waiting for approvals or second-guessing each other's capabilities. When team members trust each other's expertise and judgment, they can move forward confidently, streamlining the decision-making process.

In organizations where trust is lacking, decisions are often delayed by hierarchical approval processes, doubt, and a fear of failure. A high-trust environment reduces these barriers, allowing teams to act decisively and respond to changes in real time.

Enhanced Collaboration and Innovation

Agile thrives on collaboration, and trust is the fuel that makes collaboration possible. Teams that trust each other are more likely to share ideas, provide feedback, and work together to solve complex problems. Trust reduces the fear of being judged or blamed, encouraging team members to speak up and contribute innovative solutions.

According to research from the *Journal of Applied Psychology*, trust is a key driver of team creativity and innovation. In agile environments, where experimentation and iteration are crucial, trust allows teams to explore new possibilities without fear of failure.

Greater Resilience in Times of Change

Organizations that foster trust are more resilient in the face of uncertainty. Trust provides a foundation of stability during periods of change, allowing teams to navigate challenges with confidence. Leaders who trust their teams to adapt and perform in the face of disruption empower them to respond proactively rather than reactively.

During crises or rapid changes, teams in high-trust environments are better able to maintain focus, communicate openly, and pivot as needed. This agility is critical to staying competitive in fast-moving markets.

Call to Action for Building Trust

Building trust is a continuous process that requires conscious effort and consistency from leaders. Trust isn't something that can be demanded—it must be earned over time through transparency, integrity, and genuine support for the people you lead. As you look to strengthen your leadership, consider the following steps to build trust within your team and organization:

Communicate Transparently: Make openness a cornerstone of your leadership style. Share the big picture with your team—both the successes and the challenges—and encourage honest feedback. When people feel like they have a complete understanding of their role and the organization's direction, trust naturally follows.

Demonstrate Integrity in Every Action: Trust is built when words align with actions. Consistency is key. Follow through on your commitments, and ensure that your decisions reflect the values and mission of the organization. Your team needs to know that they can rely on you, not just in moments of success but also in times of difficulty.

Empower Your Team: Trust your team's capabilities by empowering them to make decisions and take ownership of their work. By delegating responsibility and allowing teams to lead in their areas of expertise, you create an environment of mutual trust. Teams that feel empowered are more engaged and committed to delivering their best work.

Build Psychological Safety: Create a culture where individuals feel safe to speak up, share ideas, and take risks. Psychological safety fosters trust, which in turn fuels innovation and collaboration. As a leader, demonstrate that failure is an opportunity for learning, and encourage your team to experiment and grow without fear of judgment.

Provide Support and Accountability: Support your team with the resources and guidance they need to succeed, but also hold them accountable for results. Trust is built when teams know that their leader is invested in their success and will hold them to high standards while offering the support they need to achieve them.

By taking these steps, you can cultivate a high-trust environment where your team feels empowered to perform at their best. Trust is the foundation upon which agile practices and servant leadership thrive, enabling teams to innovate, adapt, and succeed in a rapidly changing world.

Case Study: Buffer

Overview:

Buffer, a social media management company, faced the challenge of maintaining trust, transparency, and collaboration while operating as a fully remote organization. As the company grew, the leadership team recognized that trust was the linchpin of their success. To foster a high-trust environment, Buffer implemented agile principles, radical transparency, and servant leadership practices, ensuring that teams felt empowered, connected, and supported, even across different time zones.

The transformation process involved:

- **Radical Transparency:** Buffer committed to a culture of complete openness, sharing everything from salaries and revenue numbers to internal challenges and company goals. This transparency built a foundation of trust, as employees felt included in the company's journey and confident that leadership was being honest and forthright.
- **Asynchronous Communication:** In a fully remote environment, Buffer relied heavily on asynchronous communication tools like Slack, Trello, and Notion to keep teams aligned. Trust was crucial for this approach, as employees needed to feel confident that their colleagues would complete tasks and respond without constant oversight.
- **Servant Leadership:** Buffer's leaders adopted a servant leadership model, prioritizing the needs of their teams. Leaders focused on providing support, removing obstacles, and

empowering employees to make decisions. This approach fostered mutual trust and created an environment where teams felt safe to innovate and take risks.

- **Psychological Safety:** By promoting psychological safety, Buffer ensured that employees felt comfortable sharing ideas, giving feedback, and discussing failures. Leaders openly discussed their own challenges and encouraged vulnerability, reinforcing that mistakes were opportunities for learning and growth.
- **Continuous Feedback and Adaptation:** Buffer embraced agile principles by conducting regular retrospectives and feedback sessions. Teams were encouraged to reflect on their processes, celebrate successes, and identify areas for improvement. This culture of continuous feedback strengthened trust and enhanced collaboration.

Challenges Faced:

Operating as a fully remote organization presented challenges in maintaining strong communication, alignment, and team cohesion. Initially, some employees struggled with the lack of in-person interaction and the need for self-discipline in a remote setting. Buffer's commitment to transparency, trust-building practices, and servant leadership helped overcome these challenges and foster a resilient, high-performing workforce.

Outcome:

Buffer's focus on trust and transparency led to several key outcomes:

- **High Employee Engagement:** Employees reported high levels of engagement, satisfaction, and loyalty due to the trust and autonomy they experienced.
- **Enhanced Collaboration:** Trust enabled seamless collaboration across different time zones, with teams confidently relying on each other to meet goals and deadlines.
- **Increased Innovation:** The psychologically safe environment empowered employees to propose new ideas, experiment, and take calculated risks, driving continuous improvement and innovation.
- **Sustained Agility:** Buffer's agile practices and trust-based culture allowed the company to adapt quickly to changes, maintain productivity, and remain competitive in the dynamic tech industry.

Buffer's journey highlights that trust is not just a component of agile success—it is the foundation. By prioritizing transparency, psychological safety, and servant leadership, Buffer created an environment where agility, collaboration, and innovation could thrive.

Key Takeaway:

Buffer's experience demonstrates that building a high-trust culture through transparency, psychological safety, and servant leadership enables agile teams to perform at their best. Trust fosters engagement, innovation, and adaptability, proving that it is the cornerstone of effective leadership and organizational success.

Why: Nelson Mandela's release from prison and his subsequent leadership of South Africa exemplify the power of trust. Mandela's ability to foster trust among diverse groups helped unify a nation and shows how trust can transform leadership and society.

CHAPTER 12

Leading with Empathy

*"Leadership is not about being right.
It's about making others right."*
— Dan Rockwell

Introduction

Empathy is the emotional cornerstone of servant leadership. While trust fosters collaboration and empowerment, empathy ensures that leaders truly understand and connect with the needs of their team members. Leading with empathy means more than just listening—it requires leaders to actively understand and share the feelings, challenges, and aspirations of their teams. This emotional insight fosters deeper relationships, builds loyalty, and enhances team morale.

Empathy in leadership is not only a moral imperative but also a practical one. Research shows that empathetic leaders are better at resolving conflicts, fostering innovation, and driving team engagement. In this chapter, we will explore the academic research that supports the role of empathy in leadership, as well as practical steps leaders can take to cultivate empathy in their daily practices.

Empathy in Leadership: What the Research Says

Empathy is often viewed as a "soft skill," but research from the fields of psychology and leadership studies reveals that it has a profound impact on organizational success. Empathetic leadership not only improves team dynamics but also enhances performance, creativity, and employee retention. Below, we review some key findings from peer-reviewed research that highlights why empathy is essential in leadership:

Empathy Drives Engagement and Retention

Research published in the *Journal of Business Ethics* found that employees who perceive their leaders as empathetic are more likely to be engaged and committed to their organization. Empathy fosters a sense of belonging, where team members feel valued and understood. This emotional connection increases job satisfaction and reduces turnover, as employees are more likely to stay with organizations where they feel supported.

A study by the *Center for Creative Leadership* showed that 91% of employees who work for empathetic leaders report higher levels of job satisfaction. This finding highlights how empathy leads to greater loyalty and lower attrition rates, which is crucial for maintaining a stable, high-performing team.

Empathy Enhances Communication and Conflict Resolution

Effective communication is a cornerstone of leadership, and empathy significantly enhances a leader's ability to communicate. According to a study published in the *Harvard Business Review*, leaders who demonstrate empathy are better able to listen actively and respond to team members' concerns. This creates a two-way dialogue where employees feel heard, leading to more open and honest communication.

Empathy also plays a critical role in conflict resolution. Research from the *Journal of Applied Psychology* suggests that empathetic leaders are better equipped to resolve conflicts by understanding the underlying emotions and perspectives of all parties involved. By showing empathy, leaders can de-escalate tensions, foster mutual understanding, and find solutions that benefit both the individual and the team.

Fostering Creativity and Innovation

Empathy creates a psychological safety net, where individuals feel free to express themselves without fear of judgment. According to research published in the *Journal of Leadership & Organizational Studies*, teams led by empathetic leaders are more likely to innovate and take creative risks. When team members know that their ideas will be respected and considered, they are more willing to share bold or unconventional suggestions.

In agile environments, where innovation and experimentation are critical, empathy is particularly valuable. Empathetic leaders encourage creative problem-solving by making it clear that failure is part of the learning process. This mindset of empathy-driven innovation helps teams adapt quickly, explore new solutions, and iterate effectively.

Empathy and Emotional Intelligence

Empathy is a key component of emotional intelligence (EI), a critical leadership skill. Leaders with high emotional intelligence are better at recognizing and regulating their own emotions, as well as understanding the emotions of others. Research published in the *Journal of Organizational Behavior* found that leaders with strong EI, particularly empathy, were more successful in managing teams, building relationships, and leading through change.

Empathy allows leaders to navigate complex emotional dynamics within their teams, from managing stress to motivating individuals during challenging times. It also helps leaders foster a culture of care, which is especially important in industries with high-pressure environments or fast-paced changes.

Practicing Empathy as a Leader

Empathy, while often viewed as an innate trait, can be cultivated and strengthened through intentional practices. Leaders who consciously develop their empathy not only improve their relationships with their teams but also foster a work environment where people feel understood and supported. Below are practical strategies for leaders to practice empathy effectively:

Active Listening

One of the most fundamental ways to practice empathy is through active listening. Leaders who truly listen to their team members, without interrupting or rushing to offer solutions, demonstrate that they value their team's input. Active listening involves not just hearing the words spoken but paying attention to nonverbal cues, such as body language and tone of voice, which often convey underlying emotions.

According to a study in the *Journal of Communication*, active listening increases trust between leaders and team members, as it shows genuine interest in their perspectives. Leaders can practice this by asking clarifying questions, reflecting on what they've heard, and resisting the urge to provide immediate solutions. This approach fosters deeper understanding and opens up channels for more meaningful dialogue.

Practicing Perspective-Taking

Perspective-taking is a key component of empathy. It involves imagining oneself in another person's position and considering their thoughts, feelings, and experiences. Leaders who practice perspective-taking are better able to understand the challenges their team members face, whether personal or professional.

Research in the *Journal of Experimental Social Psychology* found that leaders who engage in perspective-taking build stronger emotional connections with their teams, leading to improved morale and cooperation. Leaders can practice this by making an effort to see situations from their team members' points of view, especially during conflict resolution or when providing feedback.

Showing Compassion in Difficult Times

Leaders often encounter situations where their team members face personal or professional hardships, such as family issues, illness, or overwhelming work pressures. In these moments, compassionate empathy—where leaders not only understand the emotions of their team but also take action to help—makes a profound impact.

Compassionate leaders demonstrate that they care about their team members as individuals, not just as employees. This might involve offering flexible work arrangements, lending a listening ear, or simply acknowledging their struggle. A study in the *Journal of Compassionate Leadership* shows that leaders who respond with compassion in difficult times create a culture of loyalty and trust, reducing stress and increasing employee retention.

Giving Thoughtful and Constructive Feedback

Providing feedback is an essential leadership task, but empathetic leaders deliver feedback in a way that is both constructive and considerate of the individual's emotions. Empathy in feedback means understanding how the message might affect the recipient and framing it in a way that encourages growth without causing defensiveness or discouragement.

Empathetic feedback is solution-focused, emphasizing what can be improved rather than solely pointing out what went wrong. Leaders should also be mindful of the timing and context in which they provide feedback, ensuring it's done in private and with the intention of helping the individual succeed.

Empathy and Psychological Safety

Psychological safety is a concept that has gained prominence in leadership research, particularly in relation to high-performing teams. Empathy plays a pivotal role in creating a psychologically safe environment, where team members feel free to express ideas, voice concerns, and take risks without fear of retribution or judgment.

Building a Culture of Open Communication

Leaders who prioritize empathy foster open communication, which is the bedrock of psychological safety. In organizations where empathy is practiced, team members feel comfortable sharing their thoughts and ideas because they know they will be met with understanding and respect. According to research published in *MIT Sloan Management Review*, teams with psychologically safe environments are more innovative and resilient because employees feel free to contribute without fear of negative consequences.

Empathetic leaders promote this openness by encouraging team members to speak up and actively listening to their concerns. When individuals feel heard, they are more likely to take the risks necessary for creativity and innovation.

Encouraging Risk-Taking and Innovation

Empathy allows leaders to understand the fears and hesitations that team members may have when it comes to taking risks or suggesting new ideas. Leaders who empathize with these concerns are better equipped to create an environment where team members feel safe to take calculated risks, knowing that failure will not be met with blame but seen as a learning opportunity.

A study from the *Journal of Organizational Behavior* shows that empathetic leadership is closely linked to higher levels of innovation because employees are more willing to step outside of their comfort zones. Empathy reduces the fear of failure, which is critical in agile environments where experimentation and iteration are part of the process.

Reducing Workplace Anxiety and Stress

In high-pressure environments, workplace anxiety and stress can undermine performance and morale. Empathetic leaders who recognize the signs of stress—such as fatigue, disengagement, or burnout—can intervene before these issues escalate. Offering support, reducing workloads, or providing additional resources can help alleviate stress and restore balance to the team.

Research in the *Journal of Occupational Health Psychology* found that empathetic leadership is correlated with lower levels of employee burnout and higher job satisfaction. By practicing empathy, leaders help their teams navigate stress and maintain their well-being, which in turn enhances overall productivity.

Call to Action for Empathetic Leadership

Empathy is more than a soft skill—it is a critical leadership tool that drives engagement, innovation, and performance. Leaders who practice empathy create stronger connections with their teams, build trust, and foster a culture of openness and collaboration. Empathetic leadership empowers individuals to perform at their best, knowing they are supported and understood.

Here are practical steps for leaders to take in cultivating empathy:

1. **Develop Active Listening Habits**: Make a conscious effort to listen fully to your team members. Practice patience in conversations, ask clarifying questions, and listen to understand, not just to respond. Active listening helps you uncover the underlying emotions and motivations behind what your team members are saying.

2. **Practice Perspective-Taking Regularly**: Before making decisions or providing feedback, consider how your actions will impact others. Put yourself in your team members' shoes to gain a deeper understanding of their challenges, motivations, and emotional needs. This will help you make more empathetic, informed decisions.

3. **Show Compassion in Tough Situations**: When team members face difficulties, offer genuine support. Recognize their challenges, offer flexible solutions, and demonstrate that you care about their well-being. Compassionate leadership strengthens loyalty and deepens emotional bonds within the team.

4. **Create an Environment of Psychological Safety**: Encourage open communication and make it clear that ideas, concerns, and risks are welcome in your team. Foster a culture where failure is viewed as part of learning and growth, not as a cause for punishment. Psychological safety encourages innovation and risk-taking, essential in agile and dynamic environments.

5. **Provide Feedback with Empathy**: When giving feedback, be thoughtful and considerate. Frame your feedback as an opportunity for improvement rather than criticism. Empathetic feedback helps individuals feel supported and motivated to grow, rather than defensive or discouraged.

Empathy is a powerful leadership skill that can transform not only your relationships with your team but also the overall success of your organization. By making empathy a core part of your leadership style, you'll build a more resilient, innovative, and engaged team that is capable of thriving in even the most challenging environments.

Case Study: Microsoft's Satya Nadella

Overview:

When Satya Nadella took over as CEO of Microsoft in 2014, the company was facing internal challenges related to rigid hierarchies, internal competition, and a decline in innovation. Nadella's leadership approach—rooted in empathy—helped transform Microsoft's culture, turning it into a more collaborative, innovative, and agile organization. By emphasizing the importance of understanding and connecting with employees, Nadella fostered a culture of trust, psychological safety, and continuous learning.

The transformation process involved:

- **Listening Tours and Open Dialogue:** One of Nadella's first steps as CEO was to embark on a series of "listening tours" where he engaged with employees at all levels. He actively listened to their concerns, challenges, and ideas, demonstrating that their voices mattered. This practice of open dialogue helped him understand the emotional pulse of the organization and showed employees that they were valued.
- **Cultivating a Growth Mindset:** Inspired by Carol Dweck's concept of the growth mindset, Nadella encouraged employees to embrace learning, experimentation, and resilience. He emphasized that failures were opportunities for growth, which reduced fear and promoted a culture of innovation.
- **Emphasizing Psychological Safety:** Under Nadella's leadership, Microsoft prioritized creating an environment where employees felt safe to take risks, share ideas, and challenge the status quo. Teams were encouraged to collaborate, knowing they wouldn't be blamed for setbacks or mistakes.

- **Empathy-Driven Innovation:** Nadella's empathetic approach extended to Microsoft's customers. He urged teams to deeply understand customer needs and pain points, which led to more user-centered product development. This shift resulted in innovative solutions, such as the development of accessibility features for differently-abled users.
- **Inclusive Leadership:** Nadella championed diversity and inclusion, recognizing that a more empathetic and diverse workforce leads to better problem-solving and creativity. Programs and initiatives promoting inclusion were prioritized, helping employees feel seen and supported.

Challenges Faced:

Shifting Microsoft's culture from one of internal competition to collaboration was not easy. Employees were initially skeptical of the changes, and some struggled to adapt to the new mindset. However, Nadella's consistent empathy, transparency, and commitment to the company's transformation gradually won people over.

Outcome:

Satya Nadella's empathetic leadership led to a remarkable turnaround at Microsoft:

- **Increased Innovation:** Microsoft's renewed focus on empathy-driven innovation resulted in successful products like **Microsoft Teams**, **Azure Cloud**, and enhanced accessibility features.
- **Cultural Transformation:** Employees reported higher levels of collaboration, trust, and morale, leading to a more cohesive and resilient organization.

- **Business Growth:** Microsoft's market value soared, with the company becoming one of the most valuable firms globally.
- **Employee Engagement:** A culture of psychological safety and growth mindset led to greater employee satisfaction, creativity, and commitment.

Nadella's leadership shows that empathy is not just a soft skill but a transformative force that can drive innovation, engagement, and business success.

Key Takeaway:

Satya Nadella's empathetic leadership at Microsoft demonstrates that understanding and connecting with people's needs, challenges, and aspirations can transform an organization's culture and outcomes. Empathy fosters trust, psychological safety, and innovation, making it an essential ingredient for agile leadership and long-term success.

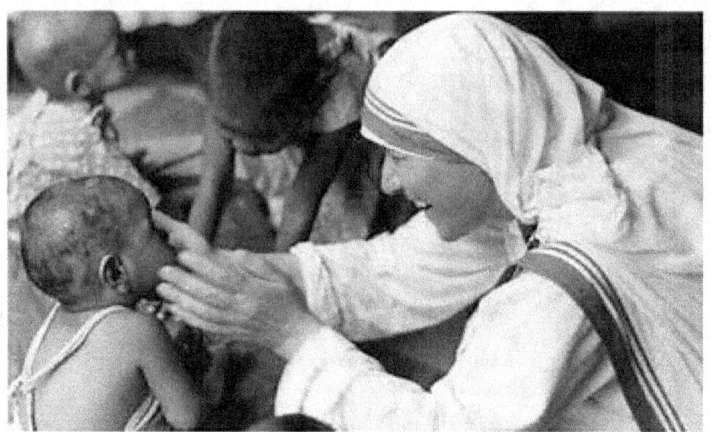

Why: Mother Teresa's life of service and compassion reflects the highest form of empathy in leadership. Her ability to connect with and serve the most vulnerable exemplifies how empathy drives true leadership.

CHAPTER 13

Empowerment as a Leadership Imperative

"As we look ahead into the next century, leaders will be those who empower others."
— Bill Gates

Introduction

Empowerment is the final pillar of the TEE (Trust, Empathy, Empowerment) philosophy and an essential element of servant leadership. While trust and empathy create the emotional foundation for strong leadership, empowerment gives teams the autonomy and responsibility they need to excel. Empowerment is about more than just delegating tasks—it involves creating an environment where team members feel confident in their abilities, supported in their decisions, and motivated to take ownership of their work.

In agile environments, where speed, adaptability, and innovation are key, empowerment is critical to success. Empowered teams can make decisions quickly, experiment with new ideas, and respond to changes without waiting for direction from leadership. In this chapter, we'll explore peer-reviewed research on the role of empowerment in leadership and organizational performance, as well as practical steps leaders can take to empower their teams.

Empowerment and Leadership: The Research

Academic research consistently highlights empowerment as a key driver of employee satisfaction, innovation, and organizational success. Empowered employees feel more motivated, engaged, and capable of making meaningful contributions to their teams and organizations. Below, we explore key findings from peer-reviewed studies on the impact of empowerment in leadership.

Empowerment Drives Motivation and Performance

Empowered employees are more motivated to perform at their best because they feel a sense of ownership over their work. Research published in the *Academy of Management Journal* found that employees who are empowered to make decisions and take initiative are more likely to be engaged, productive, and satisfied with their roles. Empowerment gives employees the autonomy they need to excel, increasing their intrinsic motivation.

The study further showed that when leaders empower their teams, performance levels improve across the board. Empowerment fosters a sense of pride and accountability, as employees are more committed to achieving high-quality results when they have control over how those results are achieved.

Empowerment Boosts Innovation

Empowerment is also closely linked to innovation. A study published in the *Journal of Applied Psychology* found that employees who feel empowered to make decisions and take risks are more likely to engage in innovative behavior. Empowered employees are not constrained by rigid hierarchies or approval processes, allowing them to experiment with new ideas, test creative solutions, and iterate quickly.

In agile environments, where innovation is essential for adapting to changing market conditions, empowerment enables teams to move quickly from ideation to execution. Teams that are given the freedom to innovate are better equipped to solve complex problems and deliver value to customers.

The Role of Empowerment in Employee Retention

Empowerment also plays a critical role in employee retention. A study in the *Journal of Leadership & Organizational Studies* found that employees who feel empowered are more likely to remain with their organizations long-term. Empowerment fosters a sense of purpose and fulfillment, as employees feel that their contributions are meaningful and valued.

In contrast, employees who are micromanaged or given little control over their work are more likely to become disengaged and seek opportunities elsewhere. By empowering their teams, leaders can reduce turnover and build a more loyal, motivated workforce.

Empowerment and Psychological Ownership

Empowerment fosters a sense of psychological ownership, where employees feel personally invested in their work and the success of the organization. According to research published in the *Journal of Organizational Behavior*, psychological ownership leads to higher levels of commitment, accountability, and performance. When employees feel that they "own" their work, they are more likely to take initiative, solve problems, and go the extra mile to achieve their goals.

Leaders who empower their teams cultivate this sense of ownership by giving employees the autonomy to make decisions and the support they need to succeed.

Empowering Your Team as a Leader

Empowering teams requires more than just assigning tasks—it involves giving employees the autonomy, resources, and confidence to make decisions and take ownership of their work. Leaders who effectively empower their teams create an environment where individuals feel motivated, valued, and capable of driving meaningful results. Here are key strategies leaders can use to empower their teams:

Delegating Authority, Not Just Tasks

Empowerment starts with delegation, but it's important to delegate more than just responsibilities—leaders must also delegate decision-making authority. When leaders trust their teams to make critical decisions, it gives team members a sense of ownership over their work. This builds confidence, accountability, and a deeper investment in the team's success.

A study published in the *Leadership & Organization Development Journal* found that employees who are given the autonomy to make decisions are more likely to engage with their work and deliver higher performance. Delegation isn't about offloading tasks; it's about empowering employees to take control of their outcomes.

Providing the Right Resources and Support

Empowering teams also means ensuring that they have the resources and support needed to succeed. Leaders must remove barriers, provide necessary tools, and offer guidance when teams face challenges. Empowerment doesn't mean leaving teams to figure everything out on their own—it's about providing a strong support system that allows teams to thrive independently.

Leaders should also offer regular feedback and encouragement, helping teams stay aligned with goals while feeling supported in their efforts. According to research from the *Journal of Applied Management and Entrepreneurship*, employees who receive both autonomy and support are more likely to take initiative and perform at their best.

Encouraging Risk-Taking and Innovation

Empowered teams are willing to take risks and experiment with new ideas because they know they won't be punished for failure. Leaders who foster a culture of risk-taking create an environment where employees feel safe to innovate, solve problems creatively, and adapt quickly to changes. Empowerment thrives in environments where teams are encouraged to step out of their comfort zones.

Leaders can promote innovation by encouraging experimentation, celebrating creative solutions, and showing that failure is part of the learning process. As highlighted in a study from the *Journal of Business Research*, organizations that empower teams to take risks are more likely to experience breakthrough innovations and continuous improvement.

Building Trust Through Empowerment

Empowerment and trust are closely intertwined. Leaders who empower their teams show that they trust their employees to make decisions, solve problems, and manage their responsibilities. This trust strengthens the bond between leaders and teams, fostering a culture of mutual respect and collaboration.

A key element of trust is giving employees room to fail without fear of retribution. When teams know they can experiment and take risks without negative consequences, they become more innovative and proactive. Empowerment builds trust, and trust, in turn, amplifies empowerment.

Empowerment and Organizational Agility

Empowerment is a crucial element of organizational agility. In agile environments, teams need the freedom and authority to make decisions quickly, respond to changes, and deliver value continuously. Empowered teams can adapt to shifting market demands, customer feedback, and internal changes with speed and confidence. Here's how empowerment drives agility in organizations:

Faster Decision-Making and Adaptation

Empowerment allows teams to make decisions without waiting for approval from higher-ups. This autonomy speeds up the decision-making process, enabling teams to respond rapidly to new information, changes in the market, or customer feedback. In agile organizations, where speed is a competitive advantage, empowered teams can pivot quickly, experiment with new approaches, and adjust course as needed.

In contrast, organizations with hierarchical decision-making processes often experience delays, as decisions must pass through multiple layers of approval. Empowerment eliminates these bottlenecks, allowing teams to take action immediately.

Increased Accountability and Ownership

Empowerment fosters a sense of ownership, where team members feel personally invested in the outcomes of their work. In agile environments, where cross-functional teams work together to deliver value iteratively, this sense of ownership is critical. Empowered teams are more likely to take responsibility for their results, ensuring that they meet deadlines, deliver quality outcomes, and continuously improve their processes.

According to research published in the *Journal of Business and Psychology*, employees who feel empowered to make decisions and take ownership of their work are more likely to hold themselves accountable and perform at higher levels. In agile organizations, where team-based accountability is essential, empowerment drives success.

Enabling Experimentation and Continuous Improvement

Agility thrives on experimentation and iteration, and empowered teams are more willing to experiment with new ideas, test different solutions, and learn from their experiences. In agile environments, empowerment encourages teams to iterate quickly, gather feedback, and refine their approach. This continuous cycle of experimentation and improvement allows organizations to stay adaptable and innovative.

Empowerment also enhances a team's ability to continuously improve by giving them the freedom to identify problems and implement solutions autonomously. Teams that feel empowered are more proactive in identifying inefficiencies, suggesting process improvements, and driving innovation.

Call to Action for Empowering Leadership

Empowering your team is a vital leadership skill that not only drives performance but also fosters innovation, engagement, and organizational agility. Leaders who empower their teams build environments where individuals feel confident, valued, and capable of making meaningful contributions. As you refine your leadership approach, consider these actionable steps for cultivating empowerment within your team:

Delegate Authority, Not Just Tasks: Empowerment is about more than assigning responsibilities—it involves giving your team the decision-making power to control how they achieve their goals. Trust your team's judgment, and provide them with the autonomy they need to take ownership of their work. Delegating authority shows that you trust their capabilities and believe in their potential.

Provide Resources and Support: Empowered teams need the right tools and support to succeed. Make sure your team has access to the resources, training, and guidance they need to excel. Offering ongoing feedback and mentorship ensures that while your team has autonomy, they also feel supported in their journey to success.

Encourage Risk-Taking and Innovation: Foster a culture where your team feels safe to take calculated risks and explore new ideas. Create an environment where experimentation is encouraged, and failure is seen as a valuable part of the learning process. By removing the fear of failure, you empower your team to innovate, solve complex problems, and adapt quickly to change.

Hold Teams Accountable While Building Trust: Empowerment does not mean relinquishing accountability. Set clear expectations and hold your team accountable for their results, while also offering the trust and support they need to succeed. This balance between accountability and trust drives ownership and commitment within the team.

Lead by Example: Demonstrate empowerment through your own actions as a leader. Model the behavior you want to see in your team by showing trust, offering guidance, and encouraging independence. Empowerment starts at the top, and when leaders embody these principles, teams are more likely to follow suit.

Empowering leadership transforms organizations by creating agile, high-performing teams that are equipped to navigate challenges, seize opportunities, and deliver exceptional results. By fostering a culture of empowerment, you'll not only elevate your leadership but also unlock the full potential of your team.

Case Study: Netflix

Overview:

Netflix, the global streaming giant, faced the challenge of maintaining agility and innovation in an industry marked by rapid technological changes and shifting consumer preferences. Under the leadership of **Reed Hastings**, Netflix embraced a culture of empowerment that gave employees the autonomy to make decisions, take risks, and drive innovation. This culture of empowerment has been a cornerstone of Netflix's success, enabling the company to stay ahead of competitors and continuously adapt to market demands.

The transformation process involved:

- **Freedom and Responsibility Culture:** Netflix implemented a unique approach known as the **"Freedom and Responsibility"** culture. Employees were empowered to make decisions and take initiative, with the understanding that they were responsible for delivering high-quality results. This approach reduced bureaucracy and allowed teams to move quickly and innovate freely.
- **Removing Approval Layers:** Netflix eliminated many traditional layers of approval, trusting employees to make decisions that aligned with the company's goals. This autonomy sped up decision-making processes, allowing teams to respond rapidly to opportunities and challenges.
- **Context Over Control:** Instead of micromanaging, leaders provided context and clear objectives, empowering employees to determine the best path to achieve those goals. By sharing information transparently, leaders ensured that teams had the knowledge they needed to make informed decisions.

- **Encouraging Risk-Taking:** Netflix fostered a culture where taking calculated risks was encouraged and failure was seen as a learning opportunity. Teams were empowered to experiment with new ideas, knowing that leadership supported innovation and learning from setbacks.
- **Continuous Feedback and Accountability:** While autonomy was encouraged, accountability was maintained through continuous feedback. Regular performance reviews and candid conversations ensured that employees understood expectations and had the support needed to succeed.

Challenges Faced:

Empowering employees required a shift in mindset for both leaders and teams. Some employees initially struggled with the high levels of autonomy and the responsibility that came with it. Additionally, maintaining alignment in a decentralized decision-making environment posed challenges. Netflix overcame these hurdles by promoting transparency, reinforcing company values, and providing ongoing support and feedback.

Outcome:

Netflix's culture of empowerment led to remarkable outcomes:

- **Rapid Innovation:** Empowered teams developed groundbreaking features like personalized content recommendations, interactive storytelling (e.g., "Black Mirror: Bandersnatch"), and high-quality original programming.
- **Agility and Adaptability:** Teams were able to pivot quickly in response to market trends, such as transitioning from DVD rentals to streaming and then to original content production.

- **High Employee Engagement:** Employees reported higher job satisfaction, motivation, and commitment due to the autonomy and trust they experienced.
- **Business Success:** Netflix's empowered culture contributed to its growth into a global leader in the streaming industry, with millions of subscribers worldwide and a reputation for innovation.

Netflix's experience demonstrates that empowerment is not just about delegation but about creating an environment where employees are trusted, supported, and motivated to take ownership of their work.

Key Takeaway:

Netflix's journey highlights that empowering teams with autonomy, context, and responsibility can drive innovation, agility, and business success. By trusting employees, encouraging risk-taking, and maintaining accountability, leaders can unlock the full potential of their teams and build a resilient, high-performing organization.

Why: Martin Luther King Jr.'s leadership empowered millions to take action for civil rights. His emphasis on empowering others to bring about change aligns with the chapter's focus on empowerment

CHAPTER 14

Becoming a TEE Leader

"The function of leadership is to produce more leaders, not more followers."
— Ralph Nader

Introduction

Trust, Empathy, and Empowerment (TEE) are not just leadership buzzwords; they are the pillars that define impactful leadership in a dynamic world. Becoming a TEE leader is not about authority—it's about influence, transformation, and sustainability. Leaders who embody these principles create teams that are not just productive but engaged, innovative, and resilient.

This final chapter serves as your call to action. Leadership is a journey, and true transformation begins with deliberate action and self-reflection. To fully integrate TEE leadership into your organization and leadership style, you must commit to continuous learning, self-assessment, and structured implementation.

The TEE Leadership Self-Assessment and Implementation Roadmap serve as critical tools to help you measure where you are today, identify gaps, and establish a clear plan for improvement. Without these, leadership transformation remains theoretical rather than actionable.

Integrating TEE Leadership into Your Daily Actions

Becoming a TEE leader requires embedding Trust, Empathy, and Empowerment into every decision, interaction, and strategic move. These principles are not just about how you lead—they define how you build future leaders. Here's how you can actively implement TEE leadership in your day-to-day role:

Building Trust Through Transparent Communication

- Regularly share updates about company goals, challenges, and progress.
- Be open about your decision-making process and invite feedback.

- Acknowledge mistakes and demonstrate accountability, fostering psychological safety.

Practicing Empathy in Leadership

- Conduct regular one-on-one check-ins beyond just performance discussions.
- Actively listen to team members' concerns and perspectives.
- Show emotional intelligence by recognizing and addressing team stressors.

Empowering Teams for Higher Performance

- Shift from directive leadership to enabling teams to take ownership of their work.
- Remove unnecessary bureaucracy and approval layers to accelerate decision-making.
- Encourage innovation by creating a safe space for experimentation and learning from failures.

These steps are not just leadership improvements—they are transformational shifts that turn managers into coaches, mentors, and enablers.

Taking the Next Step: The Role of Self-Assessment and Roadmap

Understanding the impact of your leadership requires intentional evaluation and structured implementation. This is where the TEE Leadership Self-Assessment and Implementation Roadmap become indispensable.

Why the TEE Self-Assessment is Crucial

- It identifies blind spots—where your perception of leadership may differ from how your team experiences it.
- It provides a baseline for growth, ensuring that your leadership transformation is measurable.
- It fosters accountability, reinforcing continuous improvement through data-driven insights.

Why the Implementation Roadmap is a Game-Changer

- It turns theoretical leadership concepts into daily habits and strategic actions.
- It aligns organizational goals with leadership development, ensuring sustained impact.
- It provides a timeline and structure, keeping momentum alive beyond initial enthusiasm.

By using these tools, you are not just improving your leadership—you are creating a culture of TEE leadership across your organization.

Final Call to Action: Own Your Leadership Journey

This book has provided the knowledge, frameworks, and strategies to elevate your leadership. But knowledge alone does not drive transformation—action does.

The next step is yours.

1. Take the TEE Leadership Self-Assessment—understand where you are today.
2. Engage in the Implementation Roadmap—structure your leadership transformation with clear, actionable steps.

3. Commit to growth—review your leadership practices quarterly, seek feedback, and adjust strategies as needed.

By embracing Trust, Empathy, and Empowerment, you are not just leading teams—you are creating the next generation of leaders who will carry these principles forward.

"Leadership is not about what you achieve—it's about what you enable others to achieve."

This is your opportunity to redefine leadership in your organization. Step forward, lead boldly, and inspire transformation. The future of Agile leadership starts with you.

Next Steps: Implementing the TEE Leadership Assessment and Roadmap

- Access the full TEE Leadership Self-Assessment and Implementation Roadmap in the Appendix.
- Use the tools provided to measure progress, identify gaps, and drive real leadership transformation.
- Share these insights with your team—empower others to lead alongside you.

Your leadership evolution starts now. Are you ready?

APPENDIX

TEE 360° Leadership Assessment

Introduction

This 360° review complements the TEE Leadership Self-Assessment by gathering feedback from team members, peers, and direct reports. The goal is to identify gaps between self-perception and external feedback to drive alignment and leadership growth.

Instructions:

Participants should rate the leader on a scale of 1 to 5 for each statement, where: 1 = Strongly Disagree

2 = Disagree

3 = Neutral

4 = Agree

5 = Strongly Agree

After collecting responses, compare the results with the self-assessment to identify strengths, gaps, and areas for alignment and improvement.

Section 1: Trust

1. The leader communicates openly and transparently with the team.
2. I feel comfortable approaching this leader with concerns without fear of repercussions.

3. This leader follows through on commitments and models integrity.
4. The leader actively seeks and values feedback from others.
5. I trust this leader to delegate effectively and support team autonomy.
6. This leader consistently recognizes and appreciates team contributions.

Subtotal Score (Add up responses for Section 1): _____

Section 2: Empathy

1. This leader listens actively and makes an effort to understand different perspectives.
2. The leader is aware of and considerate toward team members' emotional well-being.
3. The leader takes action to remove roadblocks and support employee success.
4. This leader fosters a culture of inclusion where team members feel heard and valued.
5. The leader demonstrates emotional intelligence in handling team dynamics.
6. I believe this leader genuinely cares about my personal and professional growth.

Subtotal Score (Add up responses for Section 2): _____

Section 3: Empowerment

1. The leader provides a clear vision and encourages autonomy in decision-making.

2. This leader encourages innovation and supports learning from failures.
3. The leader actively supports team members in their professional development.
4. I feel empowered to make decisions and take ownership of my work under this leader.
5. The leader provides the necessary tools, resources, and training for success.
6. I feel confident that my contributions are valued and respected by this leader.

Subtotal Score (Add up responses for Section 3): _____

Scoring & Comparison with Self-Assessment

Total Score: (Sum of all sections): _____

- Compare this score to the leader's self-assessment. Identify areas where perceptions align and where significant gaps exist.
- Key Questions for Analysis:
    1. Where is the leader underestimating or overestimating their effectiveness?
    2. Are there recurring themes in the feedback that indicate a blind spot?
    3. What areas do others believe the leader excels in that they may not recognize?

Gap Realization & Alignment

Step 1: Compare & Identify Gaps

- Review both self and 360° assessment scores.
- Identify the most significant gaps (3+ point differences signal strong misalignment).
- Focus on patterns rather than isolated scores.

Step 2: Align on Growth Areas

- Prioritize 2-3 key areas for development based on the biggest gaps.
- Conduct a leadership coaching session to discuss findings and create an action plan.
- Seek clarification from reviewers if needed through follow-up discussions.

Step 3: Implement & Improve

- Set clear SMART goals for improvement in the identified areas.
- Engage in peer mentoring, leadership coaching, or training as needed.
- Actively apply feedback and measure behavioral changes.

Step 4: Revisit & Measure Progress

- Reassess using the TEE 360° Leadership Review in 6 months to track growth.
- Compare new feedback with initial results to measure improvement.
- Continue refining leadership behaviors based on ongoing feedback.

Final Thoughts

The TEE 360° Leadership Assessment bridges the gap between self-awareness and external perception, driving leaders to be more intentional about trust, empathy, and empowerment. By comparing self-evaluations with team feedback, leaders gain actionable insights to enhance their effectiveness and create a positive, high-impact leadership culture.

Implementing TEE Leadership for Lasting Impact

Introduction

As we conclude this journey through Agile leadership, it is critical to move beyond theory and into action. The **TEE Leadership Model—Trust, Empathy, and Empowerment—** is not a static concept; it is a living, evolving leadership practice that requires deliberate implementation and continuous refinement. This final chapter provides the structured roadmap and assessment tools necessary to embed TEE Leadership into your organization and evaluate progress over time.

TEE Leadership Implementation Roadmap

Month 1: Laying the Foundation (Awareness & Alignment)

- Kickoff Meeting: Introduce the TEE Leadership Model to leadership and teams.
- Define Leadership Goals: Align expectations with TEE principles.
- Initial Trust & Empathy Assessment: Conduct an anonymous survey measuring current levels of trust and empathy.
- Establish Communication Channels: Set up structured feedback and transparency mechanisms.
- Leadership Self-Assessment: Leaders evaluate their current effectiveness using the TEE Self-Assessment tool.

Month 2: Building Trust

- Transparency & Communication Initiative: Implement regular leadership check-ins and town halls.
- Trust-Building Exercises: Conduct workshops focused on openness, integrity, and accountability.
- Delegation & Autonomy Training: Empower teams with increased decision-making responsibilities.
- Recognition System: Establish structured acknowledgment of contributions and successes.

Month 3: Cultivating Empathy

- Empathy Training Sessions: Interactive workshops on active listening and emotional intelligence.
- Employee Well-being Check-ins: Monthly one-on-one discussions between leaders and direct reports.
- Workload & Burnout Prevention Review: Address team stressors and implement sustainable work practices.
- Structured Feedback Loop: Encourage open, safe feedback mechanisms at all levels.

Month 4: Empowering Teams

- Decision-Making Autonomy: Shift decision-making authority to teams where appropriate.
- Growth & Skill Development Plans: Implement mentorship and professional development programs.
- Innovation & Experimentation Framework: Encourage risk-taking and iterative learning.
- Servant Leadership Integration: Leaders act as enablers, removing obstacles rather than directing tasks.

Month 5: Measuring & Aligning Leadership Effectiveness

- TEE 360° Leadership Assessment: Conduct the assessment for holistic leadership feedback.
- Analyze Gaps: Compare self-assessment and 360° results to identify key discrepancies.
- Refinement & Action Plan: Develop a leadership coaching strategy based on assessment findings.
- Recognition & Reinforcement: Celebrate leadership improvements and team progress.

Month 6: Embedding & Scaling TEE Leadership

- Institutionalizing Best Practices: Establish TEE Leadership as an ongoing leadership philosophy.
- Sustainability Strategy: Create long-term plans to maintain the culture of trust, empathy, and empowerment.
- Peer-to-Peer Recognition System: Foster ongoing accountability for leadership behaviors.
- TEE Leadership Advisory Group: Form a leadership development group to continuously assess and refine TEE principles.

Sustaining TEE Leadership Beyond the First Six Months

- Quarterly Leadership Reflection Meetings: Maintain ongoing self-improvement cycles.
- Annual Leadership Pulse Survey: Gauge long-term organizational leadership health.
- Adapt and Evolve: Adjust leadership strategies as organizational needs change.

TEE Leadership Self-Assessment & 360° Leadership Review

Self-Assessment for Leaders

This self-assessment tool enables leaders to reflect on their strengths, weaknesses, and leadership effectiveness in applying the TEE Model. Leaders rate themselves on key behaviors related to trust, empathy, and empowerment, then use the results to guide self-improvement.

360° Leadership Assessment for Team Members

To gain a well-rounded understanding, this review gathers feedback from team members, peers, and direct reports. By comparing self-assessment results with 360° feedback, leaders identify gaps between how they perceive themselves and how others experience their leadership.

Gap Realization & Leadership Alignment

Step 1: Compare & Identify Leadership Gaps

- Review both self-assessment and 360° feedback results.
- Identify the largest misalignments. A difference of three or more points in scoring indicates a significant perception gap.
- Look for trends, not isolated responses. If multiple people cite the same issue, it's a crucial area for development.

Step 2: Align & Develop Leadership Goals

- Prioritize 2-3 key areas for development based on the most significant gaps.

- Create an action plan that includes targeted leadership coaching, feedback integration, and behavioral changes.
- Schedule follow-up discussions to clarify feedback, where necessary.

Step 3: Implement & Improve Leadership Practices

- Apply learnings immediately through leadership actions and interactions.
- Participate in leadership coaching or mentorship programs.
- Encourage teams to hold leaders accountable for behavior adjustments.
- Seek peer feedback regularly to track ongoing progress.

Step 4: Revisit & Measure Leadership Growth

- Reassess using the TEE 360° Leadership Review in 6-12 months.
- Compare new results with initial findings to track development.
- Refine leadership practices continually based on emerging insights.

Final Thoughts: The Future of TEE Leadership

The TEE Leadership Model is not a one-time initiative but a sustainable, evolving framework for adaptive, people-first leadership. Leaders who embrace trust, empathy, and empowerment will create organizations that are not only agile and resilient but also deeply human-centered.

By consistently applying this roadmap and assessment framework, you will foster a culture where leadership is not about authority, but about enabling others to thrive.

The true test of leadership is not what you accomplish—it's the legacy of empowerment and growth you leave behind.

References

- **Center for Creative Leadership.** (2016). *Empathy in Leadership: What the Research Says.* Retrieved from https://www.ccl.org/articles/leading-effectively-articles/empathy-in-leadership/

- **Edmondson, A.** (1999). *Psychological Safety and Learning Behavior in Work Teams. Administrative Science Quarterly*, 44(2), 350-383.

- **Harvard Business Review.** (2018). *The Neuroscience of Trust.* Retrieved from https://hbr.org/2017/01/the-neuroscience-of-trust

- **Scrum.org.** (2023). *Case Studies of Agile Transformation.* Retrieved from https://www.scrum.org/case-studies:contentReference{index=0}

- **John Deere Case Study.** (2019). *Scaling Agile at John Deere.* Retrieved from https://www.scaledagileframework.com/case-study-john-deere-agile/

- **Prosci Change Management Certification.** (2020). *Overview of Change Management and Certification Paths.* Retrieved from https://www.prosci.com/certification/

- **Intralinks Case Study.** (2022). *Scrum Reboot: A Cultural Transformation.* Retrieved from https://www.scrum.org/case-study-scrum-reboot:contentReference{index=1}

- **Valpak Case Study.** (2020). *Scaling Agile Using SAFe at Valpak.* Retrieved from https://www.scaledagile.com/valpak-case-study:contentReference{index=2}

- **Penta Technologies Case Study.** (2021). *From Siloed Teams to Agile Excellence.* Retrieved from https://www.scrum.org/case-studies/penta-technologies-agile-transformation:contentReference{index=3}

- **Salesforce Agile Transformation.** (2018). *Agility and Growth at Salesforce. Forbes.* Retrieved from https://www.forbes.com/sites/forbestechcouncil/2018/04/15/how-salesforce-built-agility/

- **MeVis Medical Solutions Case Study.** (2019). *Improving Productivity Through Agile Practices.* Retrieved from https://www.scrum.org/case-studies/mevis-medical-agile:contentReference{index=4}

- **Microsoft Visual Studio Team Case Study.** (2017). *How Microsoft Uses Scrum to Innovate Faster.* Retrieved from https://www.scrum.org/case-studies/microsoft-visual-studio-scrum:contentReference{index=5}

- **Ling App Case Study.** (2020). *How Ling Used Agile to Transform Language Learning.* Retrieved from https://www.scaledagile.com/case-study/ling-app-agile-transformation:contentReference{index=6}

- **International Coach Federation (ICF).** (2021). *Overview of Coaching Certifications.* Retrieved from https://coachingfederation.org/credentials-and-standards

- **Certified ScrumMaster (CSM).** (2022). *Scrum Alliance Certification Overview.* Retrieved from https://www.scrumalliance.org/get-certified/scrum-master-track/certified-scrummaster

- **PMP Certification Overview.** (2022). *Project Management Professional Certification.* Retrieved from https://www.pmi.org/certifications/project-management-pmp

Appendix: Lifelong Learning in Agile Leadership

Why Continuing Education is Essential for Agile Leaders

In an ever-evolving world, agility is not only a business strategy—it's a way of thinking. As leaders in Agile environments, it is crucial to remain adaptable, continually improving both ourselves and our teams. The rapidly changing landscape of technology, market dynamics, and organizational needs demands that leaders stay at the forefront of innovation, learning new methodologies and refining their skills.

As a lifelong learner and educator, I encourage you to embrace continuous education. Learning is not a one-time achievement but an ongoing journey. The ability to learn, unlearn, and relearn is central to leadership in Agile environments. By expanding your knowledge through certifications and educational programs, you not only enhance your professional capabilities but also contribute to building more adaptive, resilient teams and organizations.

Below, I have outlined several certification paths and educational programs that will help you continue to grow as a leader, whether you are just beginning your Agile journey or are looking to deepen your expertise.

Certification Paths in Project Management and Agile

Project Management Certifications

Project Management Professional (PMP)

- **Issuing Organization**: Project Management Institute (PMI)
- **Overview**: The PMP is a globally recognized project management certification, focusing on managing people, processes, and projects.
- **Certification Path**: Meet eligibility, pass PMP Exam.
- **Costs**: PMI Member: $405 | Non-Member: $555
- **Website**: PMI PMP Certification

Certified Associate in Project Management (CAPM)

- Issuing Organization: PMI
- Overview: The CAPM is an entry-level certification for those starting their project management career.
- Certification Path: Complete 23 hours of education, pass CAPM Exam.
- Costs: PMI Member: $225 | Non-Member: $300
- Website: PMI CAPM Certification

Agile Certifications

Certified ScrumMaster (CSM)

- Issuing Organization: Scrum Alliance
- Overview: Provides foundational knowledge of Scrum and prepares individuals to become ScrumMasters.
- Certification Path: Attend a 2-day course, pass CSM Exam.
- Costs: $1,000–$2,000
- Website: Scrum Alliance CSM

Professional Scrum Master (PSM I)

- Issuing Organization: Scrum.org
- Overview: Validates fundamental knowledge of Scrum.
- Certification Path: Study, pass PSM I Exam.
- Costs: $150
- Website: Scrum.org PSM I

ICAgile Certified Professional (ICP)

- **Issuing Organization**: International Consortium for Agile (ICAgile)
- **Overview**: Focuses on understanding Agile principles and mindset.
- **Certification Path**: Attend an accredited course.
- **Costs**: $600–$1,200
- **Website**: ICAgile ICP

SAFe Agile Certifications

SAFe Agilist (SA)

- **Issuing Organization**: Scaled Agile, Inc.
- **Overview**: Provides an overview of the Scaled Agile Framework.
- **Certification Path**: Attend a Leading SAFe course, pass exam.
- **Costs**: $995–$1,500
- **Website**: Scaled Agile SAFe Agilist

SAFe Scrum Master (SSM)

- **Issuing Organization**: Scaled Agile, Inc.
- **Overview**: Focuses on the role of Scrum Master in a SAFe environment.

- **Certification Path**: Attend a course, pass exam.
- **Costs**: $995–$1,500
- **Website**: SAFe Scrum Master

SAFe Program Consultant (SPC)

- **Issuing Organization**: Scaled Agile, Inc.
- **Overview**: Designed for those leading SAFe implementation across organizations.
- **Certification Path**: Attend course, pass exam.
- **Costs**: $2,995–$3,495
- **Website**: SAFe Program Consultant

Kanban Certifications

Kanban Management Professional (KMP)

- Issuing Organization: Kanban University
- Overview: Focuses on managing and improving flow within a Kanban system.
- Certification Path: Complete KMP I and KMP II courses.
- Costs: $1,000–$2,500
- Website: Kanban University KMP

Additional Educational Paths for Agile and Leadership Mastery

Business and Management Education

Master of Business Administration (MBA)

- **Overview**: An MBA equips leaders with a comprehensive understanding of business strategy, finance, leadership, and operations.

- **Why Recommend It**: Builds well-rounded business acumen, aligning Agile leadership with broader business strategy.
- **Costs**: $20,000 to $100,000+ (varies by institution).
- **Website**: Harvard Business School MBA

Executive Education Programs

- Overview: Short, focused programs designed for senior professionals to sharpen specific leadership skills.
- **Why Recommend It**: Ideal for experienced leaders seeking to refine leadership and strategic thinking.
- **Costs**: $5,000–$25,000
- **Website**: MIT Sloan Executive Education

Leadership Development Programs

Leadership Development Program (LDP)

- **Issuing Organization**: Center for Creative Leadership (CCL)
- **Overview**: Mid-to-senior level managers focus on strategic leadership and emotional intelligence.
- **Costs**: $7,500–$10,000
- **Website**: CCL LDP

The Leadership Circle Profile

- Overview: A leadership assessment focused on emotional intelligence and personal growth.
- **Costs**: $2,000
- **Website**: Leadership Circle Profile

Professional Coaching Certifications

International Coach Federation (ICF) Certifications

- **Overview**: Globally recognized certifications for leadership coaching.
- **Costs**: ACC: $3,000–$6,000 | PCC: $6,000–$10,000
- **Website**: ICF Certification

Co-Active Training Institute (CTI) Coaching Certification

- **Overview**: Focuses on collaborative, empowering coaching techniques.
- **Costs**: $5,000–$12,000
- **Website**: CTI Certification

Data-Driven Decision-Making and Analytics

Certified Analytics Professional (CAP)

- **Overview**: Focuses on applying analytics to business decision-making.
- **Costs**: $695–$895
- **Website**: CAP Certification

Data Science Courses (Coursera, edX)

- **Overview**: Offers a range of data science, analytics, and machine learning courses.
- **Costs**: $39–$400
- **Website**: Coursera

Change Management Certifications

Prosci Change Management Certification

- **Overview**: Focused on managing organizational change using the ADKAR model.
- **Costs**: $4,500–$6,000
- **Website**: Prosci Certification

Change Management Specialist (CMS)

- **Overview**: Provides foundational knowledge of change management processes.
- **Costs**: $299
- **Website**: CMS Certification

Summary

This appendix highlights the most valuable certification paths and educational opportunities for those pursuing excellence in Agile leadership. By continuously investing in learning, you build the adaptability, skills, and mindset needed to thrive in an Agile, ever-changing world.

About the Author

Dr. Kevin Duffy is an accomplished Doctor of Business Administration (DBA), educator, Agile transformation expert, and thought leader with extensive experience in the fields of leadership, project management, and organizational change. With a deep passion for lifelong learning, Kevin combines academic excellence with practical industry insights to empower organizations and individuals to succeed in today's rapidly evolving business environment.

Throughout his career, Dr. Duffy has dedicated himself to helping companies implement Agile methodologies, improve operational efficiencies, and drive transformational change. His experience spans consulting, teaching, and public speaking, offering thought-provoking insights to a diverse range of audiences. A believer in the power of continuous education, Kevin holds multiple certifications and has developed specialized expertise in both Agile frameworks and leadership development.

Dr. Duffy's passion for teaching is reflected in his work as a professor, where he equips the next generation of leaders with the skills and mindset needed to thrive in dynamic, fast-paced environments. As an advocate for servant leadership, trust, empathy, and empowerment, Kevin is committed to inspiring positive change in organizations around the world.

When he's not speaking at conferences or consulting with organizations, Dr. Duffy enjoys sharing his knowledge through writing, where he continues to offer actionable insights for business leaders. He holds certifications in Agile, SAFe, and project management, making him a trusted advisor for organizations looking to embark on successful Agile transformations.

For more about Dr. Kevin Duffy's work, visit his website or connect with him on LinkedIn.

Glossary of Terms

Agile Terms

- **Agile**: A project management methodology focused on iterative development, collaboration, and adaptability to change.
- **Backlog**: A prioritized list of work for the development team, typically managed by a Product Owner.
- **Burndown Chart**: A visual representation of the remaining work in a Sprint over time.
- **Daily Stand-up**: A short, daily meeting where team members discuss progress, plans, and potential obstacles.
- **Epic**: A large body of work that can be broken down into smaller tasks or user stories.
- **Increment**: The sum of all completed work during a Sprint that meets the definition of done.
- **Product Owner**: The person responsible for defining and prioritizing the backlog and ensuring the team delivers value.
- **Scrum**: A framework within Agile that organizes work into fixed-length iterations called Sprints.
- **Sprint**: A time-boxed period (typically 2-4 weeks) during which a team completes a set amount of work.
- **Story Points**: A unit of measure used to estimate the relative effort required to complete a task or user story.
- **Velocity**: The amount of work a team can complete in a Sprint, usually measured in story points.

SAFe (Scaled Agile Framework) Terms

- **Agile Release Train (ART)**: A long-lived team of Agile teams that works to deliver incremental value across multiple Sprints.
- **Big Room Planning (PI Planning)**: A collaborative planning session where teams align on objectives and plan work for the next Program Increment (PI).
- **Enabler**: Work that supports the development of business functionality, like architectural work or exploration.
- **Inspect and Adapt (I&A)**: A regular SAFe event where teams reflect on progress and identify ways to improve.
- **Program Increment (PI)**: A set of iterations during which an ART delivers incremental value, typically lasting 8-12 weeks.
- **SAFe Agilist (SA)**: A certification for those who lead or support a Lean-Agile transformation in an enterprise.
- **Scrum of Scrums**: A scaled coordination meeting where representatives of multiple Scrum teams discuss dependencies and challenges.
- **Solution Train**: A group of ARTs aligned to deliver large, complex solutions.

Project Management Terms

- **Baseline**: The approved version of a project plan that represents the standard for measuring performance.
- **Change Control**: The process of managing changes to the project scope, budget, or timeline.
- **Critical Path**: The sequence of tasks that determines the shortest possible project duration.
- **Gantt Chart**: A visual representation of a project schedule, showing tasks, durations, and dependencies.

- **Milestone**: A significant point or event in the project timeline.
- **Project Charter**: A document that formally authorizes a project and outlines objectives, scope, and stakeholders.
- **Project Sponsor**: The person or group who provides resources and support for the project and is accountable for its success.
- **RACI Matrix**: A chart that defines roles and responsibilities for tasks across stakeholders (Responsible, Accountable, Consulted, Informed).
- **Risk Management**: The process of identifying, assessing, and controlling risks to the project.
- **Triple Constraint**: The balance between project scope, time, and cost, where changes to one factor typically impact the others.

www.ingramcontent.com/pod-product-compliance
Lightning Source LLC
Chambersburg PA
CBHW071529220526
45469CB00003B/706